GHOSTS

GHOSTS

Siân Evans

National Trust

CONTENTS

RIGHT A stone sphinx 'emerges' out of an ivy-covered wall at Blickling Hall, Norfolk.

> *'All houses in which men have lived and died are haunted houses: through the open doors, the harmless phantoms on their errands glide, with feet that make no sound upon the floor.'*

HENRY WORDSWORTH LONGFELLOW (1807–82)

Old buildings often have strong personalities. There is a palpable sense of place wherever people have lived and loved, and fought and triumphed and despaired. And in some old places, when the circumstances are right, the events of the past are projected onto the present, just for an instant, like electronic interference. We call these places haunted, and describe their *dramatis personae* as ghosts.

Traditionally, across all cultures and as far back as Old Testament times, ghosts have been thought to be apparitions of dead people, who appear to the living, often with a message or a dire warning for them. There is a more modern theory that what we call ghosts are not lost souls, but rather 'recordings' from former times. It is as though the present-day witnesses have glimpsed some other scene, a scenario from another time or another plane. The veil slipped for a moment, and in that interval they caught a fragment from a former era, being replayed. Those moments may be scenes of high drama, replaying a crisis in the lives of the participants, such as a murder or suicide, or the aftermath of tragedy and remorse. Alternatively, they may appear to be uneventful, mere vignettes from the everyday lives of people no longer with us, engaged in mundane activities in the places they loved and knew well.

The reasons why old places are believed to harbour ghosts are many and complex. Strong characters may 'imprint' their personalities on particular places; perhaps those sensitive enough to pick up these unconscious clues are able to detect a common impression of the forceful former inhabitants. We do not know enough about our potential to be receptive to heightened emotional states that occurred in places prior to our time, and we cannot always understand our tendency to suggestibility. But everyone has had the sensation of feeling uneasy or 'spooked' in an unfamiliar place, and even the most sceptical of people can sense strange atmospheres.

Perhaps surprisingly, almost half of people in the UK believe in ghosts, according to an NOP survey conducted in 2000. Some 42% of Britons think ghosts, phantoms and other supernatural apparitions do exist. Interestingly, the study found marked regional differences, with almost two-thirds of those in Scotland and northern England admitting to having seen or felt the presence of a ghost. Those in the South, and older people, were found to be more sceptical. What is undeniable is that ghosts, and the stories associated with them, still seem to exert a strange fascination over us.

This book evolved gradually, starting as a record of the many archaic tales connected to the unique places of historical importance or natural beauty in the care of the National Trust. With more than 20,000 buildings in its care, throughout England, Wales and Northern Ireland, as well as 700 miles of coastline and nearly 250,000 hectares of

'…these myths and legends are still a strong undertow in the tide of our folklore; they represent a rich vein in our cultural history, and they provide vital evidence of our strong oral tradition…'

countryside, woodland, beaches, mountains and moors, the charity conserves places as various as lavish historic houses and carefully tended gardens, storm-lashed lighthouses and remote farmhouses, deer-parks and neo-Classical temples, humble artisans' dwellings, wild woodlands and mountain ranges, lakes and landmarks, monuments to the Industrial Revolution and Neolithic burial mounds. Each of these places has its own personality, its own unique atmosphere, and many of them have ghost stories too.

The rich diversity of well-documented, sometimes contradictory, ghostly tales associated with National Trust sites often appear at first to be the product of 'verbal embroidery', blatant propaganda, vengeful feuds or too much home-brewed beer consumed on dark and stormy nights. But at the heart of each tale is always a grain of truth, and the best ghost stories are, in essence, imaginative accounts of the people who created and lived in these unique places – retold, interpreted and improved upon by their descendants and inheritors. Despite the occasional histrionic element, these myths and legends are still a strong undertow in the tide of our folklore; they represent a rich vein in our cultural history, and they provide vital evidence of our important oral tradition.

As the research progressed, it quickly became clear that there is no cut-off date for ghosts. If there has been a record of haunting at a particular place, there is often no particular point where it stops, when it slips into history. By going directly to the present-day custodians of traditionally 'haunted' places' – the staff, their families and friends, their volunteers and visitors – it became apparent that in many places people are still having those strange experiences. So, what started as a catalogue of archaic stories, an attempt to compile the historical folklore of particular places, rapidly became a unique oral history project, recording the inexplicable by interviewing the people best placed to recount their experiences – some of the 4,500 National Trust staff, the 40,000 volunteers, and the visitors, many of whom generously contributed their accounts.

Initially, the hundreds of people interviewed were often reticent about relating their experiences, perhaps because they feared possible ridicule, or simply because it can be alarming to have a bizarre experience in our everyday world. Most conversations started with, 'I was a total sceptic until…,' or 'I've never been interested in the paranormal, but…,' and would be followed by fascinating, enigmatic accounts of what one Property Manager describes as 'things that go bump in the afternoon'. Most of the experiences are *non sequiturs* – something odd happens in the course of a normal day or night, perhaps repeatedly, more of a subtle dislocation of the norm than a cataclysmic event. And then, that's it, till the next time. So staff and volunteers tend to regard these events as 'psychic weather'. 'That'll be the ghost, then,' they mutter philosophically.

Conditioned by the best special effects that Hollywood can provide, we have come to believe that all ghost stories have to be sensational, and that therefore any encounter with the paranormal is bound to be terrifying and threatening. Although there are some sinister and disturbing tales in this collection, and some of the interviewees certainly wouldn't want to relive their own hair-raising episode, many of the more contemporary experiences left the person involved puzzled or intrigued, rather than quaking with fear. Very few felt a place was so malign that they had to escape from it, and most seem to treat 'their' ghosts with a certain amount of pride and respect.

Investigations by both believers and sceptics are increasingly conducted at haunted sites, and such investigations often throw up fascinating detail which adds to the story. In addition, paranormal investigators occasionally seem to record genuine changes in temperature, and unexplained phenomena such as 'orbs' (spheres of light which are discernible on photographs and videos but unseen at the time). However, ghosts notoriously don't appear to order. In fact it is noticeable in this collection of tales that sightings often seem to happen when the witness is engaged in some routine or mundane task, when they are pre-occupied in some harmless pursuit. A recent scientific investigation at Hampton Court used infra-red cameras to track any disturbances happening overnight, and researchers were thrilled when the outline of a human figure appeared on their monitors, drifting along the Haunted Gallery…though they were less thrilled when the apparition opened a cupboard, extracted a vacuum cleaner, and revealed herself to be a cleaner making an early start on her chores.

It is important to be open-minded about ghosts, though perhaps you can be too open-minded. There is the tale of one slightly nervy aristocratic lady who was dragged from her sleep in a country house bedroom by the sound of heavy breathing and the increasing sensation that weights were pressing down on her. Too terrified to move, she lay rigid with fear in the dark, till in the first rays of dawn she recognised the distinctive profile of her new butler who, sleepwalking, was busy laying out a 14-piece dinner service on her eiderdown.

Yet we should always balance these 'tales of the unexpected' with the hundreds of accounts detailed in the following pages; from the Education Co-ordinator who watched in amazement as a grey wraith came through the wall and left by the window, to the curator who received a disapproving glare from the ghost of Disraeli. Then there was the cleaner who was harassed in the tea-room by the ghost of a potboy from the Civil War, the four people in Victorian clothes who suddenly appeared in a Belfast bar, the disembodied naked foot which materialised on a freshly swept floor, and the disembodied footsteps of the formidable Duchess of Lauderdale sweeping majestically down the staircase, preceded by the scent of roses….

RIGHT Bare branches of a shrub climb up stone steps at Bodnant Garden.

ABERCONWY HOUSE, CONWY

The ancient town of Conwy in North Wales has something of a reputation for its ghosts – the figure of a sentry has been seen on walking on the castle walls, and there are tales of a drowned fisherman making an unexpected appearance on the quayside.

In the centre of the town is a remarkable building, an intricate, stone and half-timbered house dating from the early fifteenth century. Aberconwy House is the only medieval merchant's house in Conwy to have survived the turbulent history of the walled town, and the oldest town-house to survive in Wales – tree-ring dating on the timbers has revealed that the original structure dates from around 1418–19. The furnished rooms illustrate daily life from different periods of the house's history.

It is the Jacobean rooms which are most prone to mystifying happenings. Staff, visitors and a couple of volunteers have reported occasional sightings of 'a gentleman in Victorian clothes'. The Custodian is more forthright, describing him as '...a tall, Fred Dibnah-like character.' He is usually glimpsed down-stairs but on at least one occasion he has appeared in the Jacobean part of the house at the end of the day, and has been into a room, from where he promptly vanishes – a physical impossibility as there is only one route in.

His appearances are often preceded by the smell of pipe tobacco and flowers. The staff refer to the figure as 'Mr Jones' because they believe him to be the ghost of a character who is known to have lived at the house, with his wife and ten children, between 1850 and 1880. The Joneses ran Aberconwy House as a Temperance Hotel and, after Mr Jones's death in 1880, his widow kept the business going until around 1910. By the 1920s it had fallen into disrepair, and the building was the first in Wales to be acquired by the National Trust, in 1934.

It appears Mr Jones is not alone – some visitors to the Jacobean part of the house have casually mentioned 'the lady standing by the fireplace.' One such visitor went on to describe a woman in Jacobean dress and added, 'She's been there since I've been in the building, but she doesn't mean any harm.'

Yet staff are not completely convinced that all of Aberconwy's spirits are benign – they have had too many instances of sudden, inexplicable draughts of icy cold, the sounds of footsteps in the night, and the Custodian has felt a heavy fire door slam in his face. Then there is the problem of missing office equipment. Items in everyday use routinely go missing from the office, turning up in highly unlikely places. 'Mr Jones is at it again...,' sighs the Custodian.

'...the Custodian is more forthright, describing him as "a tall, Fred Dibnah-like character"...'

LEFT The half-stone, half-timbered exterior of Aberconwy House.

AVEBURY, WILTSHIRE

One of the most important megalithic monuments in Europe, and spread over a vast area, Avebury has at its core an ancient, mystifying complex of archaic banks and ditches which wrap themselves around the minute village. Looming across the landscape of this World Heritage Site are a number of stone circles, formed of 'sarsen' standing stones which have been in place for up to 5,000 years, and a surviving avenue of standing stones which strike awe into the visitor.

There were once over 500 stones at this huge site, and it is believed to have been a focus of religious worship for thousands of years. Some stones were buried in the Middle Ages, perhaps because of their pagan associations, while others were broken up and used as building materials in later centuries.

Many of the stones were re-erected in the 1930s by the archaeologist Alexander Keiller. Under one of the flattened stones, Keiller and his team made a gruesome discovery – the skeleton of a man. From the coins found with him and his tools, it seems that he was helping to dig the burial pit for the stone when it toppled and fatally injured him. Also found were a pair of scissors and a lancet (for blood-letting and minor surgery). Archaeologists concurred that these were the tools in trade of an itinerant medieval barber-surgeon. The coins in his pocket dated from the 1320s, and the remains of the unfortunate barber are now in London. The stone was righted and is now known as the Barber Stone.

Also from Avebury comes a strange tale of a woman who claimed to see the site as it had been decades before. One October evening during the First World War, a rector's daughter and stalwart of the Land Army named Edith Olivier drove into Avebury for the first time. She wasn't too sure of the route, but set out from Beckhampton and was charmed by the misty avenue of looming megaliths along her route from the west. On arriving in the village, she noticed a crowd of villagers attending a faintly bucolic-looking fair. Nine years were to pass before she discovered not only had the massive avenue disappeared by 1800, but also that no fair had been held in the village since 1850.

Stories abound of local people seeing spectral figures and moving lights around the stones at night, as well as hearing phantom singing. As a result, the stones are still treated with a healthy respect. And there is a belief that buildings which have been constructed from former standing stones are subject to a poltergeist-like manifestation known as 'The Haunt'.

'…buildings which have been constructed from former standing stones are subject to a poltergeist-like manifestation…'

'...under one of the flattened stones, Keiller and his team made a gruesome discovery — the skeleton of a man...'

LEFT The standing stones of Avebury. From pagan myths through to twentieth-century sightings, the stones are home to many ghostly stories.

'I once heard that solemn tread. It had an indescribably awful and mournful sound…and affected me deeply…'

BADDESLEY CLINTON, WARWICKSHIRE

This romantic manor house, home to successive generations of the Ferrers family, was built with a moat in the fifteenth century and has changed little since the seventeenth. In the Elizabethan era it became a haven for persecuted Catholics – there are three priest-holes.

Given Baddesley Clinton's history, it isn't surprising that a number of ghost stories have grown up around the house. An elderly gentleman who had been a house guest of the Ferrers family in the 1930s remembers that when one of the dogs used to suddenly sit up and beg to no one in particular, the family joke was that he was 'begging to the ghost'.

Present-day staff members have come across unusual goings-on too. The current property manager describes himself as a 'teetotal sceptic', but even he was unable to explain one experience. One summer's evening, at around 9pm, he was alone in the house, working in the office. It was a sunny evening – perfectly still without a breath of wind – when suddenly he heard distinct, clear footsteps coming along the Upper Landing, towards his office. At first he thought

nothing of it, assuming that, for some reason, a colleague had come back into the house. The footsteps became louder, until they seemed to be right outside the closed office door… then silence. He got up from the desk and opened the door expecting to see someone, but there was no one. 'I didn't feel a chill running down my spine or anything like that – indeed there was no sense of malevolence at all – but I can't explain what I heard,' he said.

There have been many people who claim to have heard ghostly footsteps along that corridor at night, and have had the unnerving experience of seeing door handles turned by an unseen hand. In the late nineteenth century Rebecca Ferrers wrote, 'I once heard that solemn tread. It had an indescribably awful and mournful sound…and affected me deeply…It had a very weird effect to hear the handle jerked loudly within a few feet of where you are standing and see no-one.'

Some people reported seeing the figure of a man wearing a scarlet jacket with a white belt across his chest. Later, Rebecca came across a miniature of Major Thomas Ferrers of the 9th Regiment of Foot, who fitted the description exactly. He had died in 1817 falling from the ramparts of a castle

while on active service at Cambrai in France. Rebecca had a Mass said for Major Ferrers, after which the footsteps were heard far less frequently.

A ripping yarn is, wrongly, associated with the Library at Baddesley Clinton. In Tudor times, this was a first-floor chamber adjoining one end of the Great Hall. It was here that, according to the legend, Nicholas Brome, who had inherited the house in 1483, returned home unexpectedly and 'slew ye minister of Baddesley Church finding him in his plor [parlour] chockinge [chucking] his wife under ye chinne…'. The slaughtered priest's bloodstain supposedly made an indelible mark in front of the Library fireplace, but scientific analysis has since proved that the stain was actually pig's blood, and that the timbers of the room dated from at least one hundred years after the murder. Nevertheless, the murder was documented as having occurred at Baddesley Clinton, in one of the older parts of the house. Extremely humble and penitent after committing this crime of passion, Nicholas sought the pardon of both King and Pope, and gave money to the Church. In a final expiation, on his death in 1517 he was buried under the porch of Baddesley Clinton church so that he would be trodden on by all who entered.

BELTON HOUSE, LINCOLNSHIRE

The tranquil surroundings of this old house belie its numerous ghostly associations. Built in 1685–88, Belton House expresses the confidence and optimism of Restoration England. During the nineteenth century, Belton enjoyed a second golden age under the charismatic third Earl Brownlow. Fortunately for aficionados of the Restoration period, the Earl turned his back on the contemporary vogue for all things gothic and instead saw to it that both the house and garden were restored to their former Stuart splendour.

There are numerous ghostly associations here, with various reported sightings of an enigmatic Lady in Black. By contrast, there are also accounts of Belton's Bright Lady, a lady in a golden ball of light, who appears regularly in the Main Staircase Hall and is reputed to be Lady Alice Sherrard who lived at Belton in the early seventeenth century. The Queen's Bedroom would certainly seem to be the home of Belton's most infamous ghost, the Gentleman in Black, a tall individual clad in a black hat and cape. The room was used by Queen Adelaide, the widow of William IV, who visited Belton in 1841. There are also reports of a mysterious gentleman in grey.

The gentleman in black and the golden light have been seen on a couple of occasions in recent years by members of staff. And there are stories of a ghostly housekeeper who observes conservation cleaners as they go about their duties. In fact when the National Trust first took on the house, one of the ladies who worked for the family claimed to particularly enjoy cleaning in the Chapel Drawing Room, as she took a pride in the sensation of being scrutinised in the conscientiousness of her work!

One of the most unnerving ghost tales from Belton is associated with a framed family tree of the Brownlows, which was hanging on the wall of a dark passage at Belton House. The tree began to 'grow' another figure – the shadowy outline of a woman in period dress, complete with pearl necklace, but lacking a head…

ABOVE The Staircase Hall at Belton House where Belton's Bright Lady appears.

BENINGBROUGH HALL, NORTH YORKSHIRE

Known as the 'country house and garden of York', the present Beningbrough Hall was completed in 1716 to replace the late Elizabethan house that once stood nearby on the estate. The house was the scene of a notorious murder, though accounts differ as to whether this took place in the 1670s or 1760s. The ghost of the victim was reported to haunt the scene of this crime of passion for generations afterwards.

A fictionalised account of the murder survives in the form of an anonymous 1836 Gothic novel, *Beningbrough Hall: A Tale of the Eighteenth Century*. According to the tale, the housekeeper, Marion, was romantically involved with the gamekeeper, Martin Giles. The affair caused jealousy in the household, and the Steward of the estate, a man called Philip Laurie, urged a local poacher called Vasey to murder Marion and throw her body into the River Ouse, presumably in order to implicate their joint enemy and Philip's rival in love, the gamekeeper.

But the poacher was caught later breaking into the gamekeeper's cottage. Surprisingly perhaps, he confessed to the murder and was hanged at York, while Philip Laurie committed suicide. Did the ghost of Marion, said to walk the banks of the River Ouse seeking justice, drive them to these extreme ends?

More recently, one of the volunteer room stewards, a former policewoman, was disconcerted to glimpse through the glass panel in the front door a vaguely familiar-looking figure in a tweed jacket in the entrance hall, next to the piano. Once inside the house she discovered that there was in fact no one there who looked anything like the person she had seen. She realised that the man she had spotted had borne an uncanny resemblance to a member of the Dawnay family who had lived at the house in the early twentieth century, familiar to her only from old photographs.

RIGHT Beningbrough Hall – a view along the whole length of the south front from the State Dressing Room.

'… a man called Philip Laurie, urged a local poacher called Vasey to murder Marion and throw her body into the River Ouse…'

'…The key is still missing and this particular door has remained unopened for many years. The figure had vanished without a trace…'

BERRINGTON HALL, HEREFORDSHIRE

Elegantly situated above a broad valley with spectacular views of the Brecon Beacons, Berrington Hall exudes an air of quiet confidence and with a rich aesthetic appeal typical of the best Georgian country houses. The slightly austere-looking house, which was designed by Henry Holland and built in 1783, is tempered by one of 'Capability' Brown's most attractive landscape parks.

As might be expected of a property which encapsulates the values of the 'Age of Reason', there appear to be no ghost stories associated with the house – the late Lord Cawley was certain on that subject. However, there have been a number of reliable reports of mysterious sightings in the grounds and outbuildings within the last decade, especially around the area which houses the stable block.

The current gardener relates how, on one occasion in the late 1970s, in full daylight, he was working in the grounds by his workshop when he spotted a figure unlocking the door to the stables. The gardener realised that this was unusual as the key had been missing for some years. Puzzled, because he didn't recognise the man as one of his colleagues and it was a day on which Berrington Hall was closed to visitors, he went to investigate – only to find the stables completely locked up and deserted. He checked with other staff, none of whom had been near the stables. The key is still missing and this particular door has remained unopened for many years. The figure had vanished without a trace.

More recently, in 1995, two cleaners who had just been taken on asked the Property Manager if, after work, they could go and look at the two horses in the stable block, which they had seen through the open door on their way in. They were assured that there were no horses on the premises and

hadn't been for a considerable number of years. The cleaners refused to go through the stable arch again.

There are two theories which may partially explain these odd apparitions, and both lie in the history of the house in the first half of the twentieth century. The first Lord Cawley altered this wing of Berrington around 1900–04 to create the present stable block, and all the male members of the family were keen horsemen. Tragically, three of his four sons were killed in action in France during the First World War.

During both World Wars, parts of Berrington Hall were used as a hospital for wounded and recuperating soldiers, who would be encouraged to take gentle exercise as part of their rehabilitation. Riding would have been considered an excellent aid to recovery of both body and mind. So perhaps the glimpses of a striding figure heading for the stables, and the two horses in the looseboxes, are traces of an earlier event, picked up by sympathetic figures from our own times.

'A captive, I in this dread Tower, scenes of childhood recall,
They comfort bring in this dark hour, now gaiety hath flown,
Through Blickling's glades I fain would ride, soft green sward
Sequestered shade, no cruel intrigues to deride my simple rustic day…
…Oh, were I still a child in stature small
To tread the roselined paths of Blickling Hall.'

FROM A POEM WRITTEN BY ANNE BOLEYN,
WHILE AWAITING EXECUTION IN THE TOWER OF LONDON

BLICKLING HALL, NORFOLK

Blickling Hall in Norfolk features some of the country's most famous phantom figures. The present Jacobean house stands on the site of a former medieval manor which was the home of the young Anne Boleyn, who became Henry VIII's second wife and was doomed by her inability to bear him a male heir. Already the mother of the future Queen Elizabeth, Anne suffered the consequences of Henry's frustration when she miscarried a son, and he ordered her execution in 1536. Anne Boleyn's unhappy ghost is said to wander the grounds of Blickling in the form of the Grey Lady.

Every year on the evening of 19 May, the anniversary of her execution, the ghost of Anne Boleyn is reputed to drive up to Blickling in a coach drawn by a headless horseman, with her own head in her lap. As the coach arrives at the front door of the house, it vanishes into thin air. Tradition also has it that when news of Anne's death reached Blickling, four headless horses were seen dragging the body of a headless man – this apparition is alleged to have crossed twelve bridges in Norfolk in a single night.

There are numerous tales of less dramatic sightings of the Grey Lady in and around the house. Lord Lothian was the last private owner of Blicking prior to its acquisition by the National Trust in 1942, and it was his pragmatic and unshockable butler who spotted Anne by the lake one evening. He described her as wearing a long grey dress with a lace collar and a white mop cap. When he inquired whether she was looking for someone, she replied, 'That for which I search is lost for ever.'

In 1970 two delivery men drove up to Blickling Hall to return a painting which had been sent to specialists for conservation and cleaning. There were only two staff on duty in the house that day, and they directed the men to the Dining Room, while they struggled to relock the outer doors. The delivery men returned to the entrance and, on being asked if they needed a signature to acknowledge receipt of the painting, one replied, 'Oh, the lady signed for it…the lady in the Dining Room.' The Administrator asked to see the paperwork, on which no signature could be seen, but both the men were adamant that although she hadn't spoken to them, the lady, who was 'dressed old-fashioned, with something white around the neck' had taken receipt of the

painting and signed for it. On investigation the Dining Room was found to be empty – as was the whole building, apart from the four mystified men. Against the wall was propped the newly-returned painting – the famous Ditchley portrait of Elizabeth I, Anne's only child.

If legend is to be believed, Anne is not the only ghost in residence at Blickling. Sir John Falstofe (the inspiration for Shakespeare's Falstaff) is also thought to haunt the house and grounds. Similarly, it has been claimed that the dying groans of Sir Henry Hobart, the 4th Baronet, mortally wounded in a duel in 1698, can be heard emanating from the West Turret Bedroom on the anniversary of his death, 21 August. The room retains a forbidding presence; the pet dog of one of the staff would never willingly enter the room, but would stand on the threshold with its hackles raised, wincing and snarling. This bedroom certainly seems to be the focus of some unearthly goings-on; during the Second World War, it was occupied by an RAF Commanding Officer who was constantly frustrated and puzzled by his inability to make any of the three doors in the room stay closed.

*'...both she and her daughter have occasionally felt someone or
something gently touching their hair, as though stroking it...'*

BROCKHAMPTON ESTATE, WORCESTERSHIRE

According to the current Property Manager, Les Rogers, Lower Brockhampton Manor House is haunted by a Grey Lady, and many visitors have encountered her in an upper room. Les has never seen her with his own eyes, though he has been aware of a sudden drop in temperature and the sensation of someone standing next to him in the corner of the main bedroom. Often her appearances are preceded by a very sweet smell. Others have seen her, and they have all described a woman in Victorian dress; recently, a six-year old girl, the daughter of an estate worker, was playing alone on the lawn when she was approached by the 'Lady' who apparently asked her if she was well and what she was doing, before walking across the grass, through the gatehouse and across to the chapel... this on a day when the estate was closed to the public.

A former member of staff who was living alone on the premises recalled a number of disturbing experiences at Brockhampton, including the sensation of someone getting into bed next to her and putting an arm around her. Each time it happened she would protest vigorously – and the sensation would stop. She might have put it down to imagination, had it not been for the odd reaction of her Alsatian dog, who would stare fiercely into what appeared to be empty space, hackles rising. She would also find all doors unlocked, although she had scrupulously locked up the night before. The Visitor Services Manager has experienced some similar strange sensations – both she and her daughter have occasionally felt someone or something gently touching their hair, as though stroking it.

On a clear but frosty evening last winter, Les and a number of sceptical guests conducted a light-hearted experiment. Using a variety of cameras, they took a sequence of photographs both inside the house and outside the gatehouse. When the photos were returned, they were surprised to see that they had captured a number of inexplicable misty forms. Les describes himself as 'normally very sceptical – if I can see something, or touch it, or smell it, I'm happy.' But he is at a loss as to how to account for these forms.

Despite these odd experiences, Lower Brockhampton is described by the people who know it best as a happy house. There is always a warm welcome from the present – and, it would seem, from the past.

RIGHT A vertiginous view of the Georgian Staircase at Buckland.

BUCKLAND ABBEY, DEVON

Tucked away in its own secluded valley, Buckland Abbey was once a great monastery, the last Cistercian foundation in England, established in 1278. Following Henry VIII's Dissolution of the Monasteries in the 1530s, Sir Richard Grenville bought the abbey, and his grandson, another Richard, created a comfortable if idiosyncratic house out of the 13th-century abbey church, rather than using the domestic buildings of the community. As a result, the interior of the house is a strangely atmospheric blend of monastic architectural features adapted to secular uses.

Sir Richard's grandson was an ambitious soldier with plans to colonise the New World, but he was never able to secure royal patronage for his schemes – unlike his great rival, Sir Francis Drake. Disillusioned (it was at the refusal of the Queen to endorse his plans that he returned to Devon and converted Buckland Abbey in 1576), the younger Richard sold Buckland Abbey to Drake in 1580. Drake was delighted to make it his home, after his triumphant return to England as a hero following his epic three-year circumnavigation of the globe in the *Golden Hind*. Drake wanted a house that would reflect his newfound status, and it was from here that he planned the attack against the Spanish Armada.

Drake's famous drum, which accompanied him on his voyages around the world, can still be seen in Buckland Abbey. The myth states that when on his deathbed in Panama in 1596, Drake ordered that the drum be sent back home to Buckland Abbey, and vowed that if anyone should beat upon the drum when England was in danger, he would return to defend his country. But over the years this legend has taken on a life of its own. So, it would appear, has the drum – its mysterious beat was heard on three separate occasions in the past century. The first time was in August 1914, just before the outbreak of the First World War. Four years later the sound of a drumbeat was heard on the flagship Royal Oak as the German fleet steamed into Scapa Flow to surrender. Despite extensive searches of the ship, no drum could be found. The third time was during the retreat from Dunkirk in 1940.

Drake may have been regarded by the Elizabethan Queen and court as the saviour of England, but locally he was feared and regarded as having super-natural powers. One enduring story is that Drake made a pact with the Devil to ensure England's success as the Spanish Armada approached the English coast. His ghost is now reputed to drive across Dartmoor in a black coach drawn by headless horses, preceded by twelve goblins and pursued by a pack of baying hounds – any dog that hears their unearthly baying dies instantly.

Folklorists have speculated that this legend was the origin of the *Hound of the Baskervilles* story, written by Arthur Conan Doyle in 1901. The author used regularly to visit friends who lived near Ipplepen in Devon, so he was probably familiar with local myths and ghost stories. He may well have heard the story of the local Squire Cabell who was so wicked that when he was buried the villagers interred his remains under a giant slab, to make sure he stayed put. Nevertheless the 'Wisht Hounds' (or 'eerie' hounds) are said to come to howl at his tomb.

One particular ghostly legend related to Buckland Abbey, and believed to date from the pre-Reformation era, tells the tale of a young monk and his illicit relationship with a local maid. Following the discovery of their secret liaisons and his stern admonishment by the Abbot, the unfortunate monk took his own life, possibly by drowning in the nearby carp pond. His ghost is said to walk the road between the North and South lodges of the estate in the hours after dusk each day. Although there have been no confirmed sightings, some local people continue to avoid the road during the hours of darkness, just in case.

CASTLERIGG STONE CIRCLE, LAKE DISTRICT

Castlerigg Stone Circle lies a few miles east of Keswick, just south of the old Penrith Road. The free-standing circle of megalithic stones is approximately 30 metres (100 feet) in diameter, with a further 10 stones forming an interior rectangular setting adjoining the circle. Also known as The Keswick Carles and Druid's Circle, it was acquired in 1913 by Canon Rawnsley, one of the joint founders of the National Trust.

Castlerigg is one of the most impressive stone circles in Cumbria and the site is about 5,000 years old. As you stand inside the circle, which is high up on a windswept plateau, you are surrounded by a panorama of mountains – each of the stones seems (to some eyes) to be a symbolic representation of its backdrop. It is as though the landscape is embodied in miniature, with the stone circle acting as a three-dimensional diagram or model of the land surrounding it. Officially, the number of stones is believed to be 38, but visitors often find that they cannot count them, arriving at a different number with each attempt.

Local folklore once held that Castlerigg Stone Circle consisted of men turned to stone. A stone axe and a 'clublike implement' were found here before 1855, and in 1882 an attempt to excavate the site led to the discovery of a small amount of charcoal, but no pottery or other dateable material was found.

There are a number of accounts of 'earth lights' appearing in the centre of the circle. These phenomena have been reported all over the world, including Avebury. At Castlerigg in 1919, one observer, T. Singleton, described the phenomenon in the following way:

'We saw a number of lights in the direction of the druidical circle. Whilst we watched, one of the lights came straight to the spot we were standing. At first very faint as it was approaching, the light increased in intensity. When it came close it slowed down, stopped, quivered and slowly went out.'

One imaginative explanation held to be true in some quarters is that Castlerigg Stone Circle was part of a memorial assembly place, where kings came to mourn their dead. There they would perform funeral rites to speed the passing of the departed soul.

'…However, it seems that at least one member of the Fairfax-Lucy family is still around, and occasionally she takes matters into her own hands when she objects to the way the estate is run…'

CHARLECOTE, WARWICKSHIRE

The home of the Lucy family for over 700 years, the mellow brickwork and great chimneys of Charlecote seem to sum up the very essence of Tudor England. There are strong associations with the youthful Shakespeare, who knew the house well – he is alleged to have been caught poaching deer on one of the neighbouring estates, and was fined by Sir Thomas Lucy. Smarting from the punitive amount, Shakespeare composed a scurrilous poem, one of his first, now sadly lost, about the landowner. Outraged, Sir Thomas promptly doubled the fine and Shakespeare was forced to flee to London and lie low for a while.

In 1946 Charlecote Park was given to the National Trust by Sir Montgomerie Fairfax-Lucy. The house now is displayed as it would have been in the nineteenth century with a Victorian kitchen, scullery, laundry, brewhouse and family carriages in the coach house. However, it seems that at least one member of the Fairfax-Lucy family is still around, and occasionally she takes matters into her own hands when she objects to the way the estate is run.

During her latter years, Alianore Fairfax-Lucy established a home-from-home in the Tack Room at Charlecote Park. She would walk over to the stables every day from her home in the Old Malt House at Charlecote, and gradually she turned the place from a purely utilitarian room in which horse-riding equipment was kept, into a miniature residence of her own, complete with a fire burning in the small grate and a mounted stag's head over the mantelpiece.

After Alianore's death in 1979, the National Trust wanted to preserve the Tack Room in a way which retained something of her unique personality. On investigation, the drawers in the Tack Room were found to contain a number of valuables and important documents, and it was apparent that the old lady had stored all sorts of personal items there. In one of the blanket boxes were a number of wide-brimmed hats, and one of them was indisputably the hat Alianore had worn in an old photograph taken of her riding her favourite pony; the photo was on top of the mantelpiece. It was decided to hang the hats on the stag's antlers, in a slightly jokey manner.

Days later, the Administrator realised that the hats were no longer on show, and he found them back in the blanket chest. He assumed that either the House Steward or the cleaners had mistakenly put them back into storage, so he reinstated the hats on the antlers and spoke to his colleagues about the new display. They were puzzled – none of them had touched the hats. The next morning, the hats had gone again – sure enough, they were back in the box. The Administrator was perturbed, as the Tack Room could only be reached through two locked doors. With mounting trepidation, he put the hats back on the antlers and locked up the Tack Room for the night. The following morning, he unlocked the room apprehensively. Not only were the hats back in the blanket box, but the photograph of Alianore had disappeared. Clearly, she was not amused.

CHARTWELL, KENT

Few family homes can have such a powerful sense of the personality who lived there as Chartwell, the home of Sir Winston Churchill from 1924 until the end of his life. The rooms remain very much as he left them, with pictures, books, maps and mementoes evoking the career and interests of the great statesman.

Many people, understandably, have hoped to pick up a sense of the continuing presence of the former Prime Minister, and perhaps it is wishful thinking which leads visitors to report the occasional whiff of cigar smoke emanating from the rooms as they tour the building. But in fact, the fascinating ghost story most associated with Chartwell was actually written by Sir Winston himself, and is a tale of how his own father, Randolph, appeared to him one day.

In an article entitled 'The Dream', Sir Winston gives a moving account of how he had been painting in his garden studio at Chartwell on a foggy November afternoon in 1947. He had been attempting to paint a copy of a damaged portrait of his father, and relates how he was using a strong daylight lamp and had been concentrating on replicating his father's features for about 90 minutes – 'intensely absorbed' – when suddenly he became aware of an odd sensation and there, sitting in his red leather upright armchair, was his father, just as Winston remembered him in his prime. 'He was so exactly like my memories of him in his most charming moods that I could hardly believe my eyes. I felt no alarm; but I thought I would stand where I was and go no nearer,' he wrote.

Churchill goes on to describe their subsequent conversation, in which he attempts to convey to his startled and disbelieving father all that has happened in the fifty or so years since his death. From two World Wars to political upheavals and painting, horse-racing to family gossip, income tax to India, their conversation ranges widely across the massive changes the world had seen in five decades. The tale ends with Randolph expressing his disappointment in his son by saying, 'Of course you are too old now to think about such things, but when I hear you talk I really wonder you didn't go into politics. You might have done a lot to help. You might even have made a name for yourself.' With that, Randolph takes a match to light his cigarette and strikes it, then vanishes.

This vivid tale must be taken with a pinch of salt – at the time it was written, November 1947, Winston Churchill was in his seventies, forced into reluctant semi-retirement at Chartwell and still smarting from his rejection at the hands of the British electorate two years earlier, despite having led the country through most of the Second World War. He was engaged in writing his war memoirs, so an account of the cataclysmic world events of his adult life, and ways to describe them, must have been uppermost in his mind. His wry remarks about the father's disappointment in the son's lack of achievement could be seen as heavily ironic.

However, to many it seems unlikely that a character such as Churchill would have invented a ghost story featuring his beloved, long-dead father merely to score political points. And perhaps most telling of all is the conversation he had with his daughter Sarah later that same month, when they were quietly dining together. She indicated an empty chair and asked Sir Winston, if he had the power to put anyone in that chair to join them, who would he choose? She expected him to name one of his lifelong heroes, Napoleon or his ancestor Marlborough, perhaps. Without hesitation, he replied, 'My father, of course.' Whatever the truth, the red leather armchair still sits in the painting studio at Chartwell, alongside the portrait of Randolph.

'…With that, Randolph takes a match to light his cigarette and strikes it, then vanishes…'

LEFT The Studio at Chartwell. A portrait of Lord Randolph Churchill, Sir Winston's father, sits behind a dispatch box, hat and books.

'All the rooms had been locked and alarmed all night, and any movement should have been detected...'

CHIRK CASTLE, WREXHAM

The magnificent Marcher fortress of Chirk Castle in Clwyd dates from 1310 and has a rather austere exterior, but comfortable and elegant state rooms, formal gardens, superb Adam-style furniture, tapestries and portraits. It is a delightful place to live. The Visitor Services Manager, Kenneth Anthonisz, lives on site with his wife, young son and daughter, and they have considerable experience of the other, more ghostly residents still well-established at Chirk Castle.

The Anthonisz family's apartment is located in what was the old nursery, and the sound of children scampering up and down the corridor, as well as the noise of invisible furniture being dragged around, as though by an excited bunch of children, have been heard at all hours by the family, even in the middle of the day. Though neither of the parents has ever witnessed anything, or anyone, untoward, their daughter has encountered a number of unexpected inhabitants. When she was four years old, she saw 'a lady in green pyjamas' standing in front of her bed when she woke early one morning, and the parents have since heard her chatting to someone unseen – when questioned she describes her blithely as 'the lady in the big dress'. She has never seemed anything less than perfectly comfortable with the invisible residents.

The nursery spirits seem mischievous, but in a benign and largely affectionate way; Kenneth has been woken three times in a single night by the sensation of tiny hands pulling on his bare toes, which were sticking out from the end of the bedclothes. On one occasion, Kenneth's brother was staying in their guest room and had the uncanny sensation of someone gently stroking his hair as he lay in bed.

Elsewhere in the castle, there are occasional sightings of figures from Chirk's long and exciting history. One conservation cleaner occasionally sees 'a happy man, in a brown outfit', though his identity is uncertain. Former staff have reported seeing two soldiers carrying a third on a stretcher within the castle itself. Most recently, after locking up one night, Kenneth received an automatic emergency alert summoning him to the Drawing Room. On letting himself back into the locked room he found the buzzer which activates the alarm lying out on a chair, even though it is always kept concealed in a folder. Puzzled, Kenneth reset the alarms and locked up again, but the next morning the conservation cleaner found the buzzer lying on yet another chair in the Drawing Room. All the rooms had been locked and alarmed all night, and any movement should have been detected. Kenneth has no explanation, and describes these phenomena as 'Not threatening – just unnerving!'

CISSBURY RING, WEST SUSSEX

On the highest point of a southern spur of the Sussex Downs, near Worthing, is one of the largest and most impressive Iron Age hill-forts in the country. Cissbury is an oval of 25 hectares (60 acres) enclosed by a single bank and ditch, constructed in about 260BC. The tribe that built it had to move an estimated 60,000 tons of chalk to fortify the site.

Also on this hill and underneath the fort are about 200 Stone Age flint mines, hidden away among the gorse and bracken. Some are over 12 metres (40 feet) deep with several galleries interlinking underground. In these mines two skeletons were found, one of a young woman who perhaps fell down the shaft and was accidentally killed, the other of a young man, probably a miner. The mines were already more than 2,000 years old when the fort was built over them.

The flint mines of Cissbury Ring were first excavated by General Pitt-Rivers, a charismatic and eccentric Victorian who is generally regarded as the founder of scientific archaeological field work. When excavating the flint mines he recorded one particularly ghoulish experience which occurred while he was exploring one of the galleries.

'Presently,' he writes, 'a well-formed and perfect human jaw fell down from above, and on looking up we could perceive the remainder of the skull fixed with the base downwards, and the face towards the west, between two pieces of chalk rubble.'

The area has long had a distinctly creepy reputation. One tale is of a highwayman executed at Cissbury in the eighteenth century who, before he took his last breath, vowed that he would never rest after death. His body was buried in the middle of the road but, inexplicably, the corpse kept rising to the surface and it took several strenuous attempts to inter the cadaver thoroughly. And that wasn't the end of the story – the highwayman's spectral figure was seen riding on horseback over the track where he had finally ended his career of crime. Other road-users were doubly alarmed to find that not only were they being menaced by a highwayman, but that they could drive straight through the apparition. Coach- and cart-drivers would notice that their wheels seemed to have gone over a large obstacle in the road, but when they checked there was nothing to be seen.

'…the highwayman's spectral figure was seen riding on horseback over the track where he had finally ended his career of crime…'

BELOW A chalk path winds through Cissbury Ring, along which highwaymen would have ridden, and perhaps still do.

RIGHT The main entrance of Clandon Park. Despite its grandeur, one tenant found the ghost of a lady dressed in white too threatening to continue to live there.

'A lady dressed in white had been seen walking across the garden, carrying a large, vicious-looking knife.'

CLANDON PARK, SURREY

Close to Guildford in Surrey, a magnificent Palladian mansion was constructed by the Venetian architect Giacomo Leoni around 1730. The client was Thomas, the second Lord Onslow, who planned to replace the family's old Elizabethan mansion with the *sine qua non* in architecture, an out-standing collection of rooms beautifully decorated in exuberant baroque style.

Despite the splendour of the interior, with its double-height marble hall and exquisitely modelled plasterwork, in the nineteenth century one of the tenants refused to live there any longer, claiming that the property was haunted. A lady dressed in white had been seen walking across the garden, carrying a large, vicious-looking knife. She was challenged by a number of servants, but advanced remorselessly, at which point one of the servants, bolder than the others, fired a pistol at her – only to watch in amazement as, untouched and apparently unaware, the figure walked straight through a wall and disappeared.

More than twenty people witnessed this apparition and it was believed that the ghost was that of the first lady of the house, an extremely wealthy heiress called Elizabeth Knight, who had drowned herself in the lake, though why she should be bearing a knife defied explanation. On another occasion, Elizabeth is said to have walked through the front wall of the house, then appeared in every room, before dematerialising through the back wall.

A visitor was intrigued when she spotted a beautiful woman in a ballgown walking up the stairs in 1897. Intrigue turned to astonishment when the figure evaporated before her eyes. Elizabeth is also believed to have appeared in the Palladio Room, where she was seen by soldiers during the First World War, when the house was used as a hospital.

In more recent times, staff have reported a strong smell of flowers in an attic room where a maid had reputedly hanged herself. In the grounds, a male ghost is also believed to haunt the area – distinguishable by his considerable facial hair – and there have been reports of another female spirit, this time dressed in black.

'My life is my own, but my Standard is the King's...'

CLAYDON HOUSE, BUCKINGHAMSHIRE

The Verney family has continuously occupied Claydon House for more than 380 years and the spirit of one of them, Sir Edmund Verney, who died in 1642, apparently refuses to leave. The house was rebuilt in the eighteenth century, after which Luke Lightfoot made his mark with his extravagant and luxurious interiors. No wonder Sir Edmund still enjoys a visit – Lightfoot's designs make Claydon a little bit of heaven on earth.

Sir Edmund Verney was born in 1590 and, despite disapproving of the policies of King Charles I, and alienating his own son, a committed Parliamentarian, his personal loyalty to the monarch was so strong that he served as the Standard Bearer to the King at the disastrous Battle of Edgehill in 1642, at the advanced age of 52. Sir Edmund killed 16 Parliamentarians on the battlefield before being overcome. Captured and murdered by Cromwell's men, Sir Edmund was still clutching the Royal Standard, a symbol of his undying loyalty, as he sank to his death. The Roundheads cut off his hand to show they had regained the Standard.

His body was never recovered, but the hand, identified by a signet ring, was placed in the crypt of Middle Claydon Church. Over the centuries there have been numerous reported sightings of Edmund's distraught ghost wandering the first floor of Claydon, or standing on the stairs, and his disembodied hand is said to knock on closed bedroom doors at night.

A slightly more benign spirit has also been reported at Claydon. Florence Nightingale's sister married into the Verney family, and the Lady with the Lamp was such a frequent and honoured guest at the house that she retained her own bedroom there. The bedroom now contains memorabilia reflecting her life. Later guests have been startled by the nocturnal appearance of a lady in a long grey dress in and around Florence's old bedroom.

'No, wild mares would not at present take me away from Clouds Hill. It is an earthly paradise, and I am staying here until I am qualified for it.'

T. E. LAWRENCE, IN A LETTER TO LADY ASTOR, SHORTLY BEFORE HIS DEATH IN 1935

CLOUDS HILL, DORSET

In 1923, a tiny, isolated whitewashed brick and tile cottage in Dorset became home to T. E. Lawrence (Lawrence of Arabia). This charismatic personality, a legend of the First World War, needed a retreat from military life at nearby Bovington Camp, and from his unwanted fame. The rooms are austere and atmospheric, and virtually as he left them following his sudden death, in a motorcycle accident nearby.

Two months after his discharge from the RAF in 1935, Lawrence was severely injured when, riding back to his beloved house on his powerful Brough Superior motorcycle he swerved to avoid two errand boys on bicycles in a country lane. He died six days later in hospital. Lawrence's spirit is believed to haunt the cottage which he had used as a refuge for the previous 12 years. Since shortly after his death, there have been many sightings – at dusk, the figure of a character in swirling Arab dress has been seen entering the humble home, though its identity is unknown. Visitors who have followed the enigmatic figure into the cottage have found themselves alone. There have also been accounts of Lawrence's friend from his Arabian fighting days, Auda Abu Tayi, being seen in the Book Room.

In addition there are a number of tales relating to Lawrence's accident itself. Several people have reported hearing the sound of a motorbike bearing down on them, but just as the vehicle should become visible, the sound stops abruptly. Certainly there is some mystery about the manner of Lawrence's death – the coroner described it as 'most unsatisfactory' – and rumours have grown that Lawrence's 'unquiet' spirit might cause a danger to others in the area. In 1985, to mark the 50th anniversary of Lawrence's death, a series of exorcisms was carried out at the spot where the fatal accident occurred. Since that day there have been no further reports of the ghostly motorbike.

'... it is believed that the headless body of a woman in white stalks the battlements or walls of the ruins...'

CORFE CASTLE, DORSET

A very ancient site, believed to have been first settled 6,000 years ago, Corfe Castle is a majestic, brooding ruin, towering over Corfe Castle Village. It is surrounded by a ring of 12 barrows, believed to be the Tombs of the Twelve Brides, the wives of a number of Celtic chieftains of the area.

The castle's importance came from its strategic and largely impregnable location, controlling the route through the Purbeck hills. Throughout its history, it has been a place of scheming, betrayal and subterfuge. Even kings were not immune – there is a legend that the 18-year old Anglo-Saxon heir to the throne, Edward the Martyr, may have been murdered in the grounds of Corfe Castle in AD979 on the orders of his stepmother, Queen Elfrida. She was determined to bring about the succession of her own son, Ethelred, later known as The Unready.

Elfrida's Anglo-Saxon palace was rebuilt in 1090 following the Norman Conquest, and in subsequent centuries it was riddled with high-ranking power struggles. In the Middle Ages it was one of the five Royal castles; King John kept the Crown Jewels here, as well as 22 captured Frenchmen, whom he had locked in the dungeons and left to starve to death; Edward II was imprisoned at Corfe, prior to his own horrific murder (his bones are said to be in a bank vault at nearby Sherborne); Henry VII gave the Castle to his mother, and it reverted to Henry VIII; Queen Elizabeth I sold it to her Chancellor, Sir Christopher Hatton, and it was fortified against the Spanish Armada.

During the Civil War Corfe belonged to the Bankes family, who were Royalists, and Dame Mary Bankes organised the defence of the castle in 1643 and 1645 against strenuous sieges mounted by Cromwell's Roundheads. But an act of treachery betrayed the family – the castle was overrun, and as a punishment it was subsequently blown up by engineers from the Parliamentarian side. The sound of a child weeping can occasionally be heard nearby, and it is believed that the headless body of a woman in white stalks the battlements or walls of the ruins – she is thought to be the person who betrayed the besieged Royalists, bringing about the ruin of both the family and their formidable fortress. In addition, there are contemporary accounts of the ghostly figure of a Roundhead soldier seen in the shop stockroom, and the tea-room is said by some to be haunted.

RIGHT Queen Anne's Room at Cotehele, which formed part of the supposedly 'occupied' King Charles Room.

'…But as he struggled to remove a gold ring from one of the fingers, the body stirred…'

COTEHELE, CORNWALL

Cotehele is an early Tudor house of granite and slatestone, built mainly between 1485 and 1539 and set above the Tamar valley, which formed the main trade route through Cornwall. It was home to the Edgcumbe family for centuries, and is richly atmospheric with huge fireplaces and sumptuous textile hangings. The house's extensive gardens overlook the richly planted valley garden below, with medieval dovecote, a Victorian summer-house, and eighteenth-century tower. The house and grounds are reputed to be haunted, with occasional sightings of misty figures, and mysterious wafts of an attractive but unidentifiable herbal scent in the Punch Room.

The best-known story associated with Cotehele is of a lady who really did 'come back from the dead'. In 1671 Richard Edgcumbe married Lady Anne Montagu, but in 1675 she died and her body was deposited a few days later in the family vault. The evening after the ceremony, the sexton entered the vault, intending to open the coffin and rob the body of any valuables. But as he struggled to remove a gold ring from one of the fingers, the body stirred. Howling with fear, the sexton abandoned his lantern and ran away. Lady Anne realised where she was and, with commendable *sang-froid*, picked up the grave-robber's lantern and walked back to the house, where her unexpected reappearance presumably provoked mixed feelings. She lived on happily at Cotehele for a further 44 years – the subsequent career of the sexton is not known.

One recent visitor who claimed to be psychic detected the presence of a young man wearing a ruff in the King Charles Room. This room seems to be a particular paranormal hot spot – indeed, some people refuse to enter, asking 'What happened in there?' and describing the atmosphere is 'cloying'. Uncorroborated claims have been made that Charles I slept here in 1644, and the room is certainly furnished as it would have been in the era of the doomed monarch, though it was partitioned around 1700 in order to create the Queen Anne's Room.

One member of staff, who is sceptical about the existence of ghosts, felt the sensation of a 'warm air' pocket in the corner of the Hall on a very cold wintry day. She was busy removing the acid-free tissue from a suit of armour in preparation for when the house would reopen to visitors after the winter when suddenly the air around her became very warm, and then reverted to its chilly temperature. She also recalls that someone who was staying at the holiday cottage accommodation at Cotehele claimed to have seen a robed figure open the front door and bend over as if to feed birds, and then go back into the Hall, shutting the door behind them. This happened while the house was still closed, early on a Saturday morning. 'The visitor did not suspect that it was anything odd at the time,' she explained, 'and our conversation had begun with her asking, "Are you the lady we saw this morning?".'

CRAFLWYN HALL, SNOWDONIA

This rambling Victorian mansion lies on the outskirts of Beddgelert, at the foot of Snowdon, the highest mountain in Wales. Almost overgrown by dark trees and rampant shrubbery, Craflwyn Hall acquired a reputation in the last century for being haunted and there are a number of stories which reflect its melancholy atmosphere.

The heyday of the house was in the 1880s and 1890s, when it was the country home of Llewelyn Sidney England Parry. He inherited the property and lived there with his wife and family, developing it as a fashionable country estate, suitable for a gentleman of considerable means who liked to entertain his well-heeled friends. But in 1895 he sold the house to the first of a succession of owners; each time the house changed hands, it seemed to suffer a reverse of fortunes, and gradually it fell into a decline. In the first half of the twentieth century, the shortage of manual labour, the rise in taxes and the economic downturn caused by the Great Depression exacerbated the situation and it became increasingly difficult for the owners to manage both the house and the surrounding estate.

In the 1960s, Craflwyn's fortunes were partially revived when the house was bought by David Nemrow, a taxi-driver from Manchester who'd won the pools and was able to fulfil his lifelong ambition of owning a wonderful old house in the heart of Snowdonia.

Despite the Nemrows' windfall, by 1990 the money had all dried up, and Mr and Mrs Nemrow were gradually forced to close up individual rooms and retreat to a single living room, kitchen and bedroom. Outside the house, giant rhododendrons advanced closer every year, cutting out all daylight so that the building seemed perpetually swathed in gloom, even on sunny days. From the closed-up part of the house Mr and Mrs Nemrow began to notice disturbing noises night after night, as if in protest at the enveloping melancholy, so much so that they became reluctant to explore the shuttered rooms. One night, when Mrs Nemrow had dozed off in a chair in the kitchen, she suddenly woke to see a handsome woman in a floor-length red silk Victorian gown, which she described as 'all shimmery', standing before her. As she stared incredulously, the vision slowly dissolved into thin air. Mrs Nemrow was convinced that it was Mrs Parry, whose features were familiar to her from a formal portrait of the society hostess which hung on the walls in the sequestered part of the house.

By the time the National Trust bought the estate in 1994, the building was virtually subsumed by vegetation. As one member of staff put it, 'The sun never shone on it, it was always somehow in shadow.' So when a young man asked if he could volunteer to gain some conservation work experience, Craflwyn seemed an ideal project for him. The plan was that during the day he would work on the grounds, and at night sleep in Mr and Mrs Nemrow's former quarters, which would add to the security of the hall. Delighted, the young man moved in, setting up a camp-bed in the kitchen. The following morning, however, he complained that he hadn't slept all night. The nocturnal noises from the rest of the house had prevented sleep, but he also reported a sensation of creeping horror, as though some malevolent force was prowling the house. The sympathetic Property Manager who had arranged his work experience reassured him that all old houses creak and groan at night, especially those as dilapidated as Craflwyn, with its rotting beams, water damage, and holes in the roof. But, he promised, he would drop in at the house mid-evening to see how the volunteer was getting on. When he did so, the Property Manager was forced to think again. 'I have never felt such a spooky atmosphere in my life,' he said. 'The whole house seemed somehow poisonous, decaying. The volunteer was sitting bolt upright on his camp-bed, rigid with fear, not daring to close his eyes for an instant.' The following morning, the ashen-faced young man rolled up his sleeping bag and gratefully returned to his normal life.

Since those days Craflwyn Hall has been completely restored and refurbished – visitors can tour the grounds and the house itself provides accommodation for groups or volunteers on working holidays. So perhaps the presence of armies of conservation experts, builders and craftsmen, and the sociable nature of those staying there, has mollified the old place, lightening the atmosphere and taking it back to the glory days of the High Victorian era.

ABOVE The exterior of Craflwyn Hall. Now restored, its previous existence as a ramshackle, abandoned house coincided with many creepy stories.

'The screams would chill the blood of those who heard them ...'

CRIER OF CLAIFE, LAKE DISTRICT

The 'Crier of Claife' is a hidden quarry area on the west shores of Lake Windermere. It is in an area of steeply wooded hillside that also incorporates Forestry Commission land, and farm land, and is known as Claife Heights. In the eighteenth century a fearsome ghost that terrorised the area with its chilling screams was finally put to rest by an exorcising priest.

The ghost would call across Lake Windermere on stormy nights for the ferry which was moored on the opposite shore. Locals believe the ghost was the unquiet spirit of a medieval monk from an outpost of Furness Abbey who broke his vows by falling in love with a woman of easy virtue, who rejected him. Despairing of both his worldly happiness and the future of his immortal soul, he died of madness and despair on Claife Heights.

The screams would chill the blood of those who heard them, but on one occasion the ferryman on the east shore believed that the howls meant he had a fare, and he ventured across the lake. When he returned he was struck dumb with terror and his hair had turned white. He died the following day, unable to reveal what had terrified him to the point of death. As a result the ghost was exorcised by a priest who lived on one of the islands of Lake Windermere, and its spirit confined to the quarry and woods. It is believed the voice can still be heard on windy nights, and there have been reports of walkers being followed by a hooded figure in the vicinity of the quarry, usually as dusk falls.

'… perhaps the most imposing is the 7-foot high figure of a man clad in a leather jerkin, believed to be the ghost of Owain Glyndwr…'

CROFT CASTLE, HEREFORDSHIRE

Croft Castle near Leominster was the property of the 'famous and very Knightly family of the Crofts' since Domesday, except for an interval of 170 years – it was sold by the family in around 1750, then bought back in 1923. Croft was originally a simple castle, square in design and with a central courtyard. With its ancient walls and four round corner towers in pink stone, plus later additions and fortifications, it is no surprise that Croft is reputed to be the most haunted house in the Midlands, with a total of seven spectres supposedly in residence. Of these, perhaps the most imposing is the 7-foot figure of a man clad in a leather jerkin, believed to be the ghost of Owain Glyndwr, the Welsh freedom-fighter, from whom the Croft family are descended. He has been seen in a number of locations within the castle, especially in the Oak Room, though the apparition quickly fades. No less a figure than His Grace the Archbishop of Sydney visited Croft Castle in the late 1930s, and reported having seen the ghost of Owain Glyndwr there.

Members of staff have reported hearing inexplicable noises – the cleaners have heard the piercing wail of a crying baby many times – and there have been reports over the years of a vision of a man wearing a grey doublet and hose on the west stairs. Then there's the lady in a crinoline and close-fitting cap with long ringlets, seen gazing from a window over the east door. Legend has it that she spent end- less hours there, waiting for mail from a member of the Croft family in Ireland who was sending regular remittances home, but the letters and the allowance dried up and the woman and her small child suffered increasing privations as a result.

There was a particularly unsettling episode when a temporary member of staff had an Australian friend staying in the visitors' flat in the East Wing. As the staff member entered the room where her friend was sitting, he leapt to his feet and asked to be introduced to her 'friend', a lady in a grey dress who he claimed had followed her into the room. There was no one there.

'...the lakeshore is thought to be home to a number of particularly ancient ghosts...'

THE CROM ESTATE, CO. FERMANAGH

On the shores of Upper Lough Erne, the Crom Estate is one of Ireland's most important nature conservation areas. It is among the largest areas of semi-natural oak woodland remaining in Ireland, and the lake is one of the most important freshwater habitats in the British Isles. Ancient lichens and the diversity of plants and animals suggest that part of these woodlands may date back to before the New Stone Age, when wildwood covered most of the British Isles. And along with rare botanical survivors such as yellow iris, purple loosestrife and wild angelica, the lakeshore is thought to be home to a number of particularly ancient ghosts.

From the early eighteenth century to the 1960s, local people have told tales of a ball of light which appears from time to time hovering above the surface of Upper Lough Erne. The lake is too deep and not sufficiently stagnant to produce marsh gas, so the usual conditions known to create the phenomenon known as a 'will o' the wisp' can be discounted in this case. Some think it is evidence of a 'fianna', a ghostly revenant of the fair-headed people who originally dwelt in this area – one gentleman claims to have been watched by just such a figure, standing motionless on the shore. Others offer a more prosaic answer, that the lights are created by smugglers to deter the curious from interfering in their nocturnal activities – Crom is no more than a few miles from the border with the Republic and, until comparatively recently, illicit trade in contraband was discreetly conducted in both directions across this mysterious stretch of open water.

More recently, the lake provided two visitors with a highly disturbing experience. In 1992, a man and his wife hired a boat from the visitor centre and set off for a row around the lake. Seeking to explore, they landed on the island of Inishfendra. The day was hot, the island deserted and the husband tired from the exertion of rowing. He lay down on a flat rock which juts out over the water for a brief snooze in the sun but moments later was fully awake, panic-stricken to find himself lying on his back surrounded by a group of bare-chested, heavily armed men staring down at him. He described their loose, roughly-woven trousers, with strange cross-gartering binding the legs from ankle to knee. The figures were gone in an instant.

The couple rowed back to the visitor centre in record time. 'He looked completely ashen,' recounted the volunteer who dealt with the couple when they stumbled thankfully ashore. 'I asked if he had had some kind of funny turn.' As he told the story, the volunteer realised that the sunny spot where he had paused for a rest was known to be a votive stone, a sacred place where pre-Christian Celts used to pray and perhaps make small sacrifices to their gods. Had the visitor unwittingly blundered into a place sacred to the people who used to live there, or did he merely have a vivid dream, fired by auto-suggestion...?

CROWN LIQUOR SALOON, BELFAST

One of the finest surviving examples of a High Victorian public house, the Crown Liquor Saloon on Great Victoria Street in the centre of Belfast is richly atmospheric, with its decorative woodwork and tiles, stained glass and gas lighting in the old bar. The 'snugs' are individual wooden booths, affording a certain amount of privacy, and vaguely reminiscent of old-fashioned railway carriages. Indeed, the pub started out as a railway tavern built to cater for travellers using the Great Northern Railway terminus across the street, but in 1898 the landlord Michael Flanagan remodelled the interior, employing Italian craftsmen who were working on Belfast's Catholic churches to create the engraved mirrors and windows, tiles and mosaics.

Like many old pubs, it has a reputation for being haunted, in this case by the ghosts of former customers. Recently one visitor from England was sitting in one of the empty booths, waiting for her friends to arrive prior to a celebratory night out, when she suddenly realised she was not alone – sharing the 'snug' with her were three men and a woman, all in Victorian dress. The apparitions were fleeting, but she is convinced that she had been given a momentary glimpse into a scene from the Crown Liquor Saloon's unique history.

'... she suddenly realised
she was not alone...'

RIGHT The heavily decorated woodwork, rich ornamentation, gas lighting and snugs all lend the Crown Liquor Saloon a ghostly air.

DINEFWR, CARMARTHENSHIRE

Located on the outskirts of the attractive market town of Llandeilo in Carmarthenshire, once the capital of South Wales, this magnificent eighteenth-century landscape park was earlier home to many famous Welsh kings and nobles, including Hywel Dda and the Lord Rhys. The medieval deer-park has beautiful old trees, a herd of one hundred fallow deer and the celebrated Dinefwr White Park cattle. Paths through the estate give superb views over the Towy Valley and there is also access to Dinefwr Castle, which is run by CADW (Welsh Historic Monuments).

At the heart of the park is Newton House, a seventeenth-century building enveloped in a Victorian Gothic façade. Following extensive restoration, it is now open and contains an exhibition explaining the significance of Dinefwr in Welsh history. Some people have reported inexplicable sensations and experiences at Newton House, and although no trace of a ghost occurred when a TV crew stayed overnight to try to capture evidence in the 1980s, one of the cameramen claimed to have had the sensation of invisible hands squeezing his throat.

Staff have heard muffled men's voices when they know themselves to be alone in the house; electric lights switch themselves on and off when the house is locked up; and from time to time there is an unmistakable but mysterious aroma of pipe or cigar smoke, which is reputed to emanate from the ghost of a former family member. Each time the staff try to arrange a ghost watch, something happens to prevent it – '…like the last time, when the ceiling fell in!' as one house steward recalls. There are also a number of 'cold spots' which can be unpleasant to walk through. 'I just say, "It's only me, I'll be gone in a minute," and quickly leave!' explains the house steward.

Could it be the ghost of Lady Elinor Cavendish, believed to be either the first cousin or sister of the lady of the house in the 1720s? Lady Elinor was betrothed to a man she didn't love, and to escape him she sought refuge with her family at Dinefwr. Her enraged suitor followed her to the estate and murdered her – by strangling her in the room where the cameraman felt invisible hands at his throat...

BELOW The Victorian Gothic mansion of Newton House and the surrounding landscape of Dinefwr Park.

'… her body was never recovered. But on stormy nights, it is said, she can be seen in the mist above the entrance to Ogof Gwenno…'

DOLAUCOTHI GOLD MINES, CARMARTHENSHIRE

These unique gold mines were established 2,000 years ago by the Romans, and have been continuously mined ever since. For a long time locals thought the mines were caves. One of the mines is called Ogof Gwenno, Ogof being Welsh for caves. Gwenno is short for Gwenllian, a woman who lived at Ynys-y-Borde near Trecastle, Brecon.

The legend says that she used to bathe in the water in this mine as it was reputed to have medicinal qualities, and to be particularly good for rheumatism. One night, Gwenllian disappeared under the water and her body was never recovered. But on stormy nights, it is said, she can be seen in the mist above the entrance to Ogof Gwenno. There have also been tales of a ghost known as Ned, a mine-worker killed in an accident at Dolaucothi.

An ancient legend is attached to a massive boulder at Dolaucothi, known as the Carreg Pumsaint (the Five Saints Stone). Standing very close to the mine workings, the stone has hollows or depressions on all sides and was probably used to break up the ore-bearing stones from the goldmines. According to the legend, five saints were travelling to St David's, a major site of pilgrimage in the Middle Ages. Gwyn, Gwynno, Gwynnoro, Celynin and Ceitho had a wide reputation for sanctity and were objects of ill-will to a wicked magician who dwelt in caverns nearby, probably at Dolaucothi itself. The magician had in vain tried to bring the five into his power. One day, they happened to be passing the mines. Using black magic he raised an awful storm of lightning, thunder and hail, which beat upon and bruised the saints, so that they laid their heads against the big boulder standing near them, for shelter. But so great was the force of the hail that it beat their heads into the stone, and as they moved round to each of the sides of the stone, so the magician drove the hail to follow them, leaving the impression of their skulls on the surface of the rock. Finally he bore them away and concealed them in the innermost recesses of his cavern, and 'there they are sleeping and will not awake until King Arthur comes'.

FAR LEFT *The Head Set at the Dolaucothi Gold Mines.*
LEFT *The entrance to the mine where Gwenllian disappeared.*

'He was woken in the early hours convinced there was someone leaning over him with their hands around his throat…'

DUNHAM MASSEY, CHESHIRE

Like many great houses, Dunham Massey outside Altrincham was extensively reworked by successive generations. The original complex dates from the Tudor period, but most traces of the old manor house are now masked by the early eighteenth-century red brick building ranged around two inner courtyards. The interior blends sumptuous Edwardian decorations with exceptional Georgian furniture, paintings and Huguenot silver.

In 1938, Emperor Haile Selassie visited Dunham, and as a result the hall is a place of pilgrimage for Rastafarians, who consider the Emperor to be the head of their religion.

Like many old houses, Dunham is believed to retain the spirits of former residents. Most of the paranormal activity is reported to centre on the Oak Bedroom, which suffers from sudden inexplicable drops in temperature, possibly indicative of a supernatural appearance. A former House Steward decided to put the stories of ghostly goings-on to rest by spending the night in the bedroom. He was woken in the early hours convinced there was someone leaning over him with their hands around his throat and refused ever to repeat the exercise.

Describing himself as 'very unbelieving', the Property Manager is at a loss to explain how the Hanwell Monitor (which records changes in temperature and humidity) in the Oak Bedroom frequently records sudden, unexplained and short-lived drops in temperature, usually at 3am. 'The monitoring equipment has been both changed and checked on a number of occasions, yet it keeps happening, but only in this room…,' he explains.

Recently one evening the Property Manager and Duty Manager locked the property up for the night, set the alarms and all round had a decidedly uneventful night. The next morning they reset the alarms and unlocked the property. In the Stamford Bathroom, which is next to the Oak Bedroom, the bathsheet, normally folded over the bath, was found crumpled on the floor and damp, the bath had moisture droplets (despite the fact that, since it is a showroom only, the water supply to the room was isolated years ago) and there was visible condensation on the windows.

DUNSTANBURGH CASTLE, NORTHUMBERLAND

The magnificent ruin of Dunstanburgh Castle dominates a lonely stretch of Northumberland's beautiful coastline. As a stronghold on a basalt crag more than 30 metres (100 feet) above the crashing waves of the sea, it is believed to have been a defensive site for successive Roman and Dark Ages forces. The remains now visible date from the time of Thomas, Earl of Lancaster, who was executed there for treason in 1322, six years after he started the building work. The castle passed into the hands of his grandson John of Gaunt, but during the Wars of the Roses it changed hands many times, suffering successive waves of bombardment and damage. By the middle of the sixteenth century it had already fallen into decay.

Although the castle was never again to be home to the living, stories associated with the ruin suggest that the traces of some of its earlier inhabitants are still there. Thomas, Earl of Lancaster is believed to haunt the grounds. King Edward II had ordered his death, and the executioner took an excruciatingly inept eleven strokes to despatch him. The unfortunate Thomas is thought to stalk the grounds, bearing his own head, the face riven with an expression of horror.

One enduring tale is that of Sir Guy the Seeker, a knight who took shelter in the ruined gatehouse of Dunstanburgh on the night of a great storm. He was approached by a hideous wizard who told him of a beautiful lady who needed him to save her. He followed the wizard to a hidden chamber, where he discovered a sleeping beauty, and was told to choose between a sword and a horn to awaken and rescue her. He hesitated, picked up the horn and blew it – at which signal 100 knights in white appeared and charged towards him. When Guy regained consciousness he was alone again in the gatehouse. He became obsessed with finding the sleeping beauty again and spent the rest of his life searching the ruins. Some believe his fruitless cries can still be heard at midnight on stormy nights.

ABOVE *Dunstanburgh Castle stands aloof above the crashing waves of Whin Sill Cliff.*

'...He became obsessed with finding the sleeping beauty again and spent the rest of his life searching the ruins. Some believe his fruitless cries can still be heard at midnight on stormy nights...'

RIGHT The ruins of Dunstanburgh Castle.

RIGHT Looking through the first floor windows at Dunster Castle. Even during broad daylight Dunster Castle can seem dark and foreboding.

DUNSTER CASTLE, SOMERSET

Dunster Castle in Somerset dates from Norman times, and like many very ancient sites, has the reputation of being the haunt of many ghosts. The impressive castle seen today mostly dates from 1617 and 1870, when extensive remodelling was undertaken, although there is also a fifteenth-century gatehouse.

The shop is housed in part of the seventeenth-century stable block, and this area seems especially prone to supernatural happenings. Staff report occasional sightings of a man dressed in green who passes the door of the shop and proceeds down the stable block blithely ignoring their questions, only to disappear without trace. There are accounts of a mysterious green light that floats from the front door to the far end of the stable block, and staff are aware of a presence in the stock room opposite the shop – the shop manager has often felt quite uncomfortable when working in there.

Even in broad daylight this area is quite dark, and visitors often comment on a sense of menace at this end of the building. On five separate occasions, visitors who have felt uneasy have specifically asked if anyone had been murdered here, and one lady was adamant that two people had been murdered in the stables.

In the shop itself there are frequent, inexplicable happenings. Stock items which have been perfectly secure one minute suddenly fall over, especially displays of books at the far end of the shop. Unopened boxes of stock stored in the room have been ruined by a brown, sticky 'gunge' which appears on the innermost packets. When these were returned to the suppliers for their opinion, no explanation could be found.

Some years ago a private ghost tour of Dunster was organised for a small group of office workers from Taunton. Within the group were a number of sceptics, no doubt made bolder by the few drinks they'd imbibed before arriving at the castle for the tour. As they were standing in the stables laughing, joking and making ghostly noises, a lump of masonry, about the size of a ping-pong ball, suddenly flew down from the ceiling and struck the end stall, followed a few seconds later by a similar chunk. Even the most dismissive members of the group were decidedly unsettled by the incident and were relieved when the time came to leave the stables.

In the Blue Kitchen, a volunteer who was helping to clean the room once had a very disconcerting, inexplicable experience. This young man – who subsequently became a member of staff – was spending a couple of weeks at the castle on work experience. Whilst brushing the floor he suddenly saw a naked foot materialise between the two kitchen doorways. He described the foot as being almost transparent but as though covered in a white powder, and it faded out completely at the ankle. It took a step forward and then disappeared completely. The young man fled from the room, badly shaken by the experience, and to this day feels unhappy about entering the room alone.

The Leather Gallery owes its name to the leather hangings that depict the story of Antony and Cleopatra. In fact, the gallery formed part of the medieval castle's Great Hall and once extended through to the area which is now the Property Manager's flat. It is the most haunted room in the house, with visitations being recorded up to the present day.

The first supernatural happening to be experienced by recent house staff was in 1990, shortly after the current Property Manager and his partner had come to live at the castle. The Property Manager's mother was staying with the couple, sleeping in the East Quantoxhead suite, which is behind the door in the south wall of the castle, close to the Leather Gallery. She had gone to bed but was fully awake and reading when at 11.30pm she heard the sound of male voices in the gallery. Thinking it was her son, she decided to ask him something which had been on her mind, but then realised that the person could be another member of staff so decided against it.

The following morning she asked her son the nagging question and told him she had been going to ask him the previous night when he had been in the gallery. Puzzled, he replied that he had been in his flat all evening. Later on, he asked his colleague what he had been doing at 11.30pm – the colleague had gone to bed at his usual time of 10.30pm and had not been in the Leather Gallery at any point. And there was nobody else in the castle. Shortly afterwards, the Property Manager's partner and her brother were alarmed by the sound of a door banging at 11.40pm. Each thought the other was playing a trick on them. Then both heard numerous footsteps, followed by the low, muffled voices of a group of men, although it was impossible to make out what was being said. Neither felt brave enough to investigate. The next morning,

'…she was suddenly aware that the temperature had plummeted, and all the hairs on the back of her neck rose…'

they discovered they had separately experienced these strange phenomena at precisely the same time. Since this occurrence, several people staying in the East Quantoxhead suite have heard the same sequence of sounds at approximately the same time, and quite recently a guest reported a presence actually being in the bedroom.

At 8:30am one very hot August morning a member of the conservation cleaning staff had a distinctly unnerving encounter. She had vacuumed the wooden floorboards in the gallery and was in the process of polishing them with the electric polishing machine. It was heavy work, in intense sunlight, but as she was working towards the window she was suddenly aware that the temperature had plummeted, and all the hairs on the back of her neck rose. She was also conscious that someone had entered the room and was standing at the top of the stairs. Turning round, to her amazement she saw the shadowy figure of a man in old-fashioned military uniform standing in the doorway to the corridor. Alarmed, but with her escape route cut off, she decided that the noise from the polishing machine would scare off any ghost who had come to investigate, so she turned back and carried on. Within about 30 seconds the ice-cold feeling ceased and the temperature returned to normal. Even before she turned to look, she knew the figure had gone.

One possible explanation for these strange phenomena in that part of the house is that the Morning Room – which is just along the corridor from the gallery – was used as a dormitory for the Civil War troops when they were garrisoned here in the mid-seventeenth century. Perhaps these manifestations originate from those troubled times.

Workmen at Dunster have not been immune to its haunting qualities either. During the building works carried out in the early 1950s, two workmen were sent in to lift floorboards in order to access the heating pipes. Both men experienced a most unpleasant sense of foreboding and terror whilst doing the work, so much so that the young apprentice actually felt sick. Unable to carry on, the two men had to leave the job part way through. The apprentice recovered once he was away from the gallery but was so terrified of something unfathomable lurking there that he flatly refused to go back to the room. It was left to another workman to complete the job – he appeared to be unaffected by any presences.

Halfway up the Oak Staircase is all that remains of a mezzanine floor that once continued over the outer hall. The House Steward's flat is behind this door. Staff have often felt uneasy about this staircase, one person describing a feeling of unpleasant foreboding and talking of the oak banisters being 'wet and slippery'. She gradually became so unhappy about the atmosphere that she approached a spiritualist to exorcise what she considered to be evil spirits from the staircase, arranging for it to be done when the other house staff were absent, and telling them nothing of her plans. When the House Steward of the time returned from holiday, she remarked to her husband how cold and empty the staircase felt, so different from the usual atmosphere. The exorcism had taken place during their few days away.

The spiritualist had recorded the presence of several spirits on the staircase and in the drawing room below – indeed, the family in residence and many of their guests had related numerous sightings of a lady dressed in grey who glided up and down the staircase. The spiritualist claimed to have requested them to leave, and after long and patient persuasion they finally did so.

Dunster's Inner Hall appears to be the occasional haunt of a former volunteer Room Steward by the name of Miss Hooper. She was devoted to the castle, and especially loved spending her days talking to visitors in this room. Unfortunately, she became ill and had to give up her voluntary work, sadly passing away as a result of her illness. Yet many visitors to the Inner Hall have drawn attention to the elderly lady sitting in the steward's chair by the lamp, who disappears suddenly. Does Miss Hooper come back from time to time to look after her beloved room?

The castle's Gatehouse dates back to 1420, and would have formed part of a barbican entrance which protected the gateway. The right-hand tower contained an oubliette, or pit dungeon, now neatly tiled over. An oubliette was a place were prisoners were thrown and left to be forgotten, to die. It would have been some 7 metres (20 feet) deep, and contained the skeletons of those unfortunate souls committed to its depths during early medieval times. There is a story, said to have been verified by excavations during the late nineteenth century, that during the early 1700s an excavation of the oubliette unearthed a male skeleton, 7 feet tall and manacled by wrists and ankles to the wall, along with three or four other skeletons. In those days, someone of that height would have been a giant among men – the average height for a man would have been about 5 feet 3 inches.

Next to the Gatehouse is a flight of steps that appears to hold a particular terror for dogs. Even in daylight the steps can appear dark and gloomy, with a decidedly chilly feel. Julian Luttrell, the last of the family to live at the castle, says that on many occasions his dogs would simply refuse to use the steps, preferring to take the longer, south terrace route to reach the outside of the gateway. The present Head Gardener similarly struggles to convince his dog to climb the steps.

EAST RIDDLESDEN HALL, WEST YORKSHIRE

This atmospheric seventeenth-century manor house and its buildings are set in mature grounds with beech trees, ducks and a fishpond. The chances of bumping into a ghost are high at East Riddlesden Hall, if local folklore is to be believed. A merchant's murderer is reputed to lurk in reception, the Grey Lady walks the rooms looking for her lover, a small girl in blue weeps in a corner of the yellow porch chamber and there is even a White Lady who drowned in the pond when thrown from her horse.

The best-known ghost is believed to be the 'Grey Lady', the Tudor lady of the house who was discovered with her lover by her husband. He imprisoned her in her room, known as the Grey Lady's Chamber. The lover was walled up separately, and eventually both of them starved to death. Apparently staff and visitors have heard her footsteps running up the stairs and across the landing to her room, and the unfortunate lover is said to appear at the window of the bricked-up room where he died. On New Year's Eve every year, a 300-year-old wooden cradle in one of the bedrooms is seen to rock by invisible hands – it is rumoured to be the ghost of the Grey Lady.

In the grounds, the lake seems to be the focus of phantom appearances. A White Lady has been seen walking around the lake and she is believed to be the spirit of a woman who lived at the Hall and was supposedly thrown from her horse while hunting – her body was never found and it is thought she drowned in the lake. The fourth ghost is that of a phantom coachman, who was also thought to have been dragged into the lake by his horses. He has been seen wandering around the water, looking for his lost coach-and-four.

BELOW The remains of the Starkie Wing of East Riddlesden Hall.

FELBRIGG HALL, NORFOLK

Felbrigg Hall was built in the seventeenth century by John Windham for his son Thomas, descendants of the wealthy merchant who bought the estate in 1459. William Windham I extended the house 50 years later and in 1749 William Windham II inherited the estate.

Most of the ghost stories associated with Felbrigg are to do with a phantom bibliophile. William Windham III is believed to still visit his magnificent library, in order to read all the books he didn't have time to get through while he was alive because of the demands of political life (he was Tory Secretary for War under William Pitt from 1794–1801 and later a Whig). The ghost of the man who began Felbrigg Hall's impressive library was a scholar who loved books – nearly 200 years ago he sustained injuries trying to save precious volumes from a friend's burning library in London and died a year later following an operation in 1810.

Felbrigg's gothic library was designed by James Paine to complement the Jacobean façade. Today the fine collection of books remains – along with William Windham III's ghost, which has been observed sitting at the library table by members of staff and a volunteer. A former Property Manager also claims to have spotted him, but adds that William will only appear when an exact combination of books is on the library table. The apparition has been seen relaxing in the library chair and there is an impression of a flickering fire in the fireplace.

RIGHT The library at Felbrigg Hall housing the books collected by William Windham III and his descendents.

THE FLEECE INN, BRETFORTON, WORCESTERSHIRE

Originally a family home belonging to local farmers and dating back to the Middle Ages, The Fleece Inn at Bretforton retains a very rustic, domestic atmosphere. Lola Taplin, the granddaughter of the first publican-owner, Harry Byrd, who became the landlord in 1848, still seems to feel very much at home there. She died in 1977, but continued to remind guests that it was very much her home, and that they should treat it as such.

Lola had strong views about what was appropriate to a hostelry, and she seems to continue to make those felt in a somewhat direct manner. Licensee Peter Clark relates tales of apparitions, mysterious noises and a sinister presence from his staff and customers. Lola was always particularly averse to customers eating in the pub, and strange things have happened to people's packed lunches as a result. One unfortunate saw his sandwiches lifted into the air and dashed to the floor. 'I'd only had the one,' he said ruefully.

Since Lola's death, chairs have been seen to be rocking by themselves, sometimes with the illusion of an elderly lady sitting in them, and clocks have stopped inexplicably at 3pm. The security alarm goes off at all hours, there have been sightings of a lady in the upstairs window, lights turning on and off for no reason, and indistinct figures are seen gliding through the bar.

Of course, it may not be Lola who is behaving in such a cantankerous fashion – so old is the building that there are a number of rough circles, known as 'witches' marks', on the hearths by the fireplaces. In the days when witchcraft was a real and immediate source of fear to the majority of people, it was widely believed that witches could get into a building at night via the chimney. A charm against witches was the nightly ritual of drawing round chalk marks on the hearth so that any trespassing witch would be trapped within them until daylight. Over decades, the nightly drawing of these circles has left grooves in the hearth stones at The Fleece – testament to successive generations of fear. Peter Clark keeps an open mind over the source of the disturbances. 'The series of ancient witch circles on the floor are shrouded in mystery, but there is also a strong smell of perfume around the fireplace which nobody can explain,' he says. Given its rich history and ancient folklore, it wouldn't be surprising if the Fleece Inn had more than one resident ghost.

ABOVE A quiet corner within The Fleece. The Inn became a licensed house in 1848 and its clients have been protecting themselves from the supernatural since then.

'…since Lola's death, chairs have been seen to be rocking by themselves…'

GEORGE AND DRAGON, WEST WYCOMBE, BUCKINGHAMSHIRE

The transitory nature of pubs and inns provides the location, backdrop and stage for many human dramas, so perhaps it is not surprising that a number of them have a reputation for being haunted. One of the best known is the George and Dragon in West Wycombe, which is believed to have two ghosts.

The pub is an imposing brick building, extended and largely rebuilt around 1720, that benefited from its location on the main coach routes from London to Oxford and Aylesbury; before the advent of the railways, coaches would stop every 10 miles or so to change horses, and the passengers would have a chance to stretch their legs and break their journey, perhaps ordering a meal or drinks, provided by the innkeeper and his employees. A local serving girl at the George and Dragon was named Sukie, and she became the victim of a prank that went disastrously wrong. According to the story, she was both socially ambitious and very attractive, so when three local lads told her that they had a message for her from a wealthy gentleman admirer who was keen to meet her at dead of night in order that they elope together, she was eager to believe them. Sukie felt humiliated when no gallant appeared at the appointed time and place and, fleeing from the mocking laughter of the jokers who had hidden nearby so as to extract the maximum enjoyment from her discomfiture, she slipped and was knocked unconscious. Her tormentors carried her back to the George and Dragon, but she died later from head injuries.

It is said that the ghost of Sukie, dressed in a long white gown, occasionally appears on an upstairs landing of the

ABOVE *The coach house leading into the courtyard at the George and Dragon. Travellers have passed through the gates for centuries.*

George and Dragon, disappearing on the threshold of a particular bedroom, a room which dogs obstinately refuse to enter. Elsewhere at the inn, phantom footsteps have been heard, and they are thought to be linked to an unfortunate guest who was robbed then murdered in one of the rooms.

'…it is said that the ghost of Sukie, dressed in a long white gown, occasionally appears on an upstairs landing of the George and Dragon, disappearing on the threshold of a particular bedroom…'

GEORGE INN, LONDON

Sir Osbert Sitwell's claim that 'ghosts went out when electricity came in' is contradicted by the strange behaviour of the distrustful female ghost still believed to be in residence at the George Inn in Southwark, close to London Bridge. The George is the last galleried inn to survive in London. It stands just off Borough High Street, on the site of a previous George Inn, which burnt down in the great Southwark fire of 1676. Shakespeare is said to have acted in the courtyard of the old hostelry, and Charles Dickens wrote of it as a busy and popular coaching inn in *Little Dorrit*. As a result, historical and literary societies flocked to stage plays and gave readings in the yard, and sightseers included Winston Churchill, who brought his own port and was charged 1s 6d corkage.

The George Inn's ghost is believed to be that of either Amelia Murray or her daughter, Agnes. Amelia arrived in 1878 and together they ran the inn for more than fifty years. Both were formidable women with a growing dislike of the modern world and the trappings of progress – no bathroom was installed until after Agnes's death in 1934. The expansion of the railways ruined the trade of many old coaching inns and the George itself was under threat, with three of the four galleries demolished before a public outcry succeeded in saving what remained. Perhaps as a result, Ms Murray maintains a passionate vendetta against the trappings of modernity – electricity supplies, labour-saving gadgets and especially computers. A previous landlord commented wearily on how any new-fangled device acquired for the

George inevitably went wrong for no perceptible reason as soon as it was plugged in – it would be several weeks before the ghost would sullenly accept a new computerised till. 'Anything with a plug...' was how he put it.

A number of members of staff living on the premises have been awakened over the years to the sight of a misty female form in their rooms. Perhaps either Amelia or Agnes is still keeping a baleful eye on the running of 'her' establishment.

RIGHT The interior of the George Inn. It has been a well-loved landmark in Southwark since the seventeenth century.

'...one volunteer was startled to catch a glimpse of a woman dressed in a black Victorian costume with a white apron emerging from what is now the sitting room...'

GEORGE STEPHENSON'S BIRTHPLACE, NORTHUMBERLAND

Contrary to the stereotype, not all National Trust houses are well-appointed, lavishly decorated architectural gems. There are many places for which the historic importance far outweighs any aesthetic value, but which are valued and conserved because of the lives of their unique inhabitants.

One of Britain's greatest inventors was born in 1781 in a remote and modest stone cottage in the small colliery village of Wylam, near Newcastle upon Tyne. George Stephenson rose from extremely humble beginnings – his whole family occupied only one room at the cottage, and the young man was virtually unable to read or write until he was eighteen. As an engineer he was largely self-taught, relying on night-school classes, observation and experiment, eventually becoming the principal inventor of the railway locomotive steam engine. His invention was to have worldwide impact, revolutionising the nature of travel for individuals and facilitating the rapid transport of manufactured goods. George Stephenson provided the motive power for the mighty Industrial Revolution.

The Stephenson family left the cottage when George was eight years old, and it was subsequently lived in by a great many families who scraped a modest lived from the nearby colliery and railway. The lives of the poor and illiterate often go unrecorded, so staff at the cottage are uncertain about the identity of their resident ghost, nicknamed Mabel, but they are left in no doubt about the force of her personality.

Mabel is thought to belong to the Victorian era, and likes to make her presence felt by causing power surges and blown fuses, and by interfering with electrical gadgets such as microwave ovens. According to the current Custodian, Mabel is unusually excitable at Bank Holidays and when the house is busy during the summer months – a particularly lively burst of inexplicable incidents appears to have been triggered by one group of visitors chorusing 'Goodbye Mabel!' as they left the house, having been told the story by one of the guides.

The spare bedroom seems to be the main focal point of paranormal activity; when the Custodian moved in, for several months the room emitted a terrible smell which the best efforts of plumbers and builders were unable to eradicate. It was only when one of the plumbers jovially remarked 'You must have a poltergeist here' that the smell simply disappeared. The Custodian's long-suffering pet dog refuses to enter the spare bedroom and occasionally emits a fit of howling for no apparent reason.

The Custodian has not seen Mabel, but others have; one volunteer was startled to catch a glimpse of a woman dressed in a black Victorian costume with a white apron emerging from what is now the sitting room – she thought it might be her daughter, who also helps at the property, but as she turned to greet the figure it vanished into thin air, leaving her with a sensation of great heat and a headache which lasted all day.

Who Mabel might be, and why she should haunt the cottage, remains a mystery but staff are planning further research to try to establish her identity.

GIBSIDE, TYNE & WEAR

One of the greatest surviving examples of eighteenth-century landscape design in Britain, the Gibside estate is the former home of the late Queen Mother's family, the Bowes-Lyons, and it is the spirit of one of her ancestors who is believed to haunt the grounds. Ghostly organ music has been heard playing inside a locked Chapel, and ladies' perfume has been detected in the ruins of Gibside Hall. From time to time, an unexplained figure is seen gliding across the grass towards the Orangery – she was last glimpsed by the warden in December 2003.

One of the most famous residents of Gibside was 'The Unhappy Countess', Mary Eleanor Bowes, the Countess of Strathmore, who was born in 1749, only child of the wealthy landowner and businessman George Bowes. When her father died she inherited his large fortune and, as a result, was seen as a great prize by questing bachelors. She married John Lyon, the ninth Earl of Strathmore, and they took the joint family names of Bowes-Lyon. Mary and John were married for nine years and had children, but John became ill with tuberculosis and died at sea on the way to Lisbon to find a cure.

Mary was now a very rich widow, and a Countess. An Irish adventurer named Andrew Robinson Stoney won her heart by a series of underhand manoeuvres. The couple married but, to Stoney's horror, Mary had drawn up an 'Ante-Nuptial Trust' just before the wedding, ensuring that control of her fortune remained in her hands. Stoney was furious and treated his wife with terrible cruelty, starving and beating her, and locking her up in a cupboard in Gibside Hall. Eventually Mary escaped from her husband, and despite a failed kidnap attempt by him, lived quietly for the rest of her life.

Mary was buried in Westminster Abbey, far from the crypt of the elegant, Palladian-style chapel at her beloved Gibside.

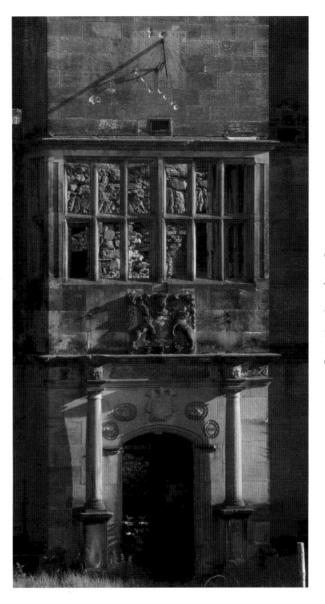

'...at one end of a great avenue of ancient oaks, the figure of a woman can sometimes be glimpsed. Is it the ghost of Mary Eleanor, fated to wander the place where she had known both great joy and sorrow?...'

But near the Gibside Orangery, at one end of a great avenue of ancient oaks, the figure of a woman can sometimes be glimpsed. Is it the ghost of Mary Eleanor, fated to wander the place where she had known both great joy and sorrow?

ABOVE AND FAR LEFT Early morning shadows are cast across the ruins of the south-east front of Gibside Hall.

71

GLASTONBURY TOR, SOMERSET

Massive and enigmatic, the curious, steep-sided Tor dominates the Somerset Levels like a dormant volcano. On the summit of the hill an archaeological excavation has revealed the remains of two superimposed churches dedicated to St Michael, of which only the tower of the fifteenth-century structure now remains.

From a distance, Glastonbury Tor looks like an island, and the earliest legends suggest that it was the sacred mount of Avalon, surrounded by water, and the home of Gwyn ap Nudd, the lord of the spirit world of Annwn. Whatever its origins, the hill has always been a holy place, dedicated to spirituality.

In the 1960s, it was claimed that there was a connection between a number of ancient sacred sites in the area – many of them had been simply adopted and adapted by the new religion of Christianity. The Tor was one of the previously pagan sites on a line between the Avebury complex in Wiltshire and St Michael's Mount in Cornwall.

More recently, theories have emerged that Glastonbury Tor is located at the meeting point of two major leylines, invisible lines of energy, each approximately 300 miles long. Known as the St Michael and the St Mary lines, for most of their length they run roughly parallel to each other, each linking places associated with each saint, so that the St Michael line, for example, connects Mont St Michel in northern France with St Michael's Mount in Cornwall, and St Michael's church on Glastonbury Tor. The lines appear to intersect at Glastonbury Tor. By using dowsing techniques, a number of experts claim to have discovered an ancient, flat labyrinth running up the sides of the Tor, like two semicircular halves of an intricate maze, which interpenetrate at the summit and encircle the surviving medieval tower. As the labyrinth descends the Tor, its contours reach out to some of the other sites linked with the area's sacred topography, some of which are associated with the Holy Grail, made famous through Arthurian legend. The truth is lost in the mists of time, but the story is strangely tenacious throughout the West Country and Cornwall.

The Tor has strong Christian associations as well. The legend has it that Joseph of Arimathea, a trader in tin and uncle to Jesus of Nazareth, brought his young nephew to the Holy Isle of Avalon, Glastonbury Tor, on one of his far-flung journeys as a merchant. Years later, after the crucifixion of Christ, Joseph returned to Avalon, moored his boat at Wearyall Hill, and stuck his staff into the ground. It took root and became known as the Holy Thorn; believers claim that the tree's direct descendant can be seen growing in the churchyard to this day. Below the hill, Joseph built a small church, dedicated to Mary, and this was reputed to be the first Christian place of worship in Britain. Joseph died at Glastonbury and was buried on nearby Chalice Hill along with the cup used at the Last Supper, an object of such importance to early Christians that many strove unsuccessfully to locate and recover the Holy Grail over succeeding centuries.

Over time, Joseph's early church grew to become Glastonbury Abbey, and by the Middle Ages this was one of the greatest monasteries in medieval Europe, attracting pilgrims wishing to venerate the relics of the saints, especially St Patrick, the patron saint of Ireland, who had died at Glastonbury in AD461. It is said that, in defiance of the Dissolution of the Monasteries under Henry VIII, the monks decided to conceal their holy relics, manuscripts and books in the subterranean caverns running under Glastonbury Tor, in the firm belief that these objects would one day be rediscovered, ushering in a new era of peace and tolerance.

To this day, strange stories are told about Glastonbury Tor. Witnesses have reported seeing coloured lights spiralling around the tower and a local police officer was at a loss to account for the sight of eight dark maroon egg-shaped objects hovering over the hill, while a later onlooker reported seeing green and violet lights dancing around the top of the tower.

The world-famous monument of Glastonbury Tor abounds with stories. To this day many celebrate it as the site of Avalon.

GREY'S COURT, OXFORDSHIRE

Charming and with a well lived-in air, Greys Court is one of those rare survivals – a country house which grew organically, from a small but tough fortified manor established in 1347, to a larger, more impressive and more opulent sixteenth-century gentleman's residence of brick and stone, built by the Knollys family during the reign of Henry VIII. Subsequent generations made some concessions to architectural sophistication, adding a seventeenth-century oriel window and an eighteenth-century wing, but overall the house remains an unpretentious and appealing amalgam of centuries of gradual evolution, rather than revolution.

There is, however, one problem – many visitors to the house remark on how cold they find it, especially in the tearoom (which is also know as the Cromwell Room, as it is believed that Cromwell's troops stayed there).

One of the volunteers currently working at Grey's Court is also a medium, and she was recently asked to intercede when one of the cleaners at the house found himself unable to enter the tearoom. The cleaner, she found, was a sensitive, rather quiet young man who was deeply troubled by the atmosphere in the room. He couldn't see anyone, but felt certain that while he was working in the room someone – or something – was trying to speak to him in some way. She asked him precisely what he had experienced, at what time of day, and told him to let her know if it happened again, so that the two of them could attempt to get to the bottom of the mystery.

Initially the cleaner was very hesitant about whether to proceed, but decided to contact the volunteer after a few days and they sat together in the empty tearoom. A spiral staircase descends into the room from the upper part of the building, and that part of the room has always seemed to be glacially cold, not only to the volunteer but also to some visitors, even though the temperature drop seems to be imperceptible to others. In fact, the cold which permeates the whole building seems to emanate from this very spot in the tea-room.

As they were sitting there, the volunteer soon became aware of the figure of a young lad, aged about 15, wearing what looked like a metal helmet set comically askew. The boy told the medium that he really wanted to talk to the cleaner, because he would understand. Both the medium and the cleaner became aware at this point of the sound of rough voices and merrymaking in the background, although only she could see the figure of the youth. He described himself as a 'potboy', an archaic term meaning a domestic servant in a tavern or inn, and plaintively remarked that 'they' bullied and teased him. In an instant both the vision and the raucous 'noises off' vanished.

'… the cold which permeates the whole building seems to emanate from this very spot in the tea-room…'

The medium associated this highly vivid apparition with the fact that during the Civil War Cromwell's soldiers stationed themselves at Grey's Court – the soldiers, or 'they', were perhaps coercing the reluctant potboy into waiting on them at table. Since the attempt to get the bottom of the strange goings-on, the cleaner has been able to go into the room alone, though the temperature hasn't noticeably improved…

HAFOD-Y-LLAN, SNOWDONIA

Snowdonia is famous for its majestic rugged landscapes, including Hafod-y-Llan on the southern flank of Snowdon itself. There is a very old farm situated in this remote spot, with a stream running down behind the farmhouse into a forbidding steep-sided gorge.

During the first half of the nineteenth century, the little community of scattered souls which made up the parish of Nant Gwynant were terrorised by an audacious thief, who would break into their isolated homes late on winter nights, stealing food and other provisions, and always managing to evade detection. Cows and goats were being milked overnight, and the best sheep were vanishing without trace. One afternoon a shepherd spotted a giant man on the hillside, enormously tall and covered in thick reddish-coloured hair. A posse of irate locals gave chase across the rough countryside but the man managed to evade capture once again.

The farmer's wife at Ty'n-yr-Owallt was particularly incensed by the regular loss of her home-made provisions. Alerted by a noise outside her kitchen at midnight, she reached in the dark for her hatchet and brought it down with all the force she could muster on an enormous figure who was stepping into the room. The intruder let out a bellow of pain and ran out into the yard. With trembling fingers the farmer's wife lit her lantern and discovered that her axeblow had severed one of the thief's hands at the wrist – but this

'... with trembling fingers the farmer's wife lit her lantern and discovered that her axeblow had severed one of the thief's hands at the wrist...'

limb was huge, thickly covered with coarse dark hair, like the pelt of an animal. Shocked but determined, the next day the locals followed the trail of blood in the snow, along the ravine to a tiny ledge which led to a cave halfway up the steep sides of the gorge. They wisely decided that discretion was the better part of valour and chose not to investigate further. From then on, there were no more unwelcome nocturnal raids, but the cave can be seen to this day and is known as Ogof y Gwr Blewog, 'The Cave of the Hairy Man'.

BELOW Fast-moving waters cascade over rocks in Snowdonia.

HAM HOUSE, SURREY

Set on a peaceful, lush bank of the River Thames, Ham House near Richmond is thought to be one of the National Trust's most prolifically haunted locations. Cold spots, sounds of footsteps, sightings of an imperious lady and a small dog, glimpses of a hurrying cleric and a profoundly gloomy young man, the inexplicable scents of roses and Virginia tobacco, and the mysterious nocturnal movements of furniture have given Ham a 'busy' reputation. A recent investigation at the house, conducted overnight by the Ghost Club, concluded that there could be as many as fifteen phantoms in residence, including a number of dogs.

Ham House was the life's work of the tenacious and strong-willed Duchess of Lauderdale (1626–98), a highly ambitious aristocrat who played a dangerous political game of intrigue with both Royalists and Puritans during the middle of the seventeenth century. By becoming a friend to both Cromwell – openly – and to Charles II (secretly), she schemed and plotted to maintain her power base and was even ruthless enough to sue her own family if they crossed her. It is her unquiet spirit which some believe roams the house to this day.

Elizabeth Murray inherited Ham House from her father in 1655. She was beautiful, but she was also described as 'restless in her ambition, profuse in her expense, and of a most ravenous covetousness'. Her first marriage in 1648 was to Sir Lionel Tollemache, a wealthy squire, but even before his death in 1669 Lady Dysart (as she then was) was rumoured to have formed an attachment to John Maitland, 1st Earl of Lauderdale, Secretary of State for Scotland. Six weeks after the death of his wife in 1672, John married Elizabeth. Ignoring outraged public opinion about the unseemly haste of the match, and dark rumours about the conveniently close deaths of both her husband and his wife, they set about extending and refurbishing Ham in luxurious style that befitted the court of Charles II.

But the Earl fell from Royal favour, and died in 1682. The Duchess found herself increasingly hard-up – she even attempted to sue her husband's brother for the cost of her husband's lavish funeral expenses, an impressive bill of £5,000. Ten years of unsuccessful litigation followed, and Elizabeth was forced to sell many of the treasures she had collected so avidly. She ended her days suffering from gout, barely able to move from room to room. She wrote 'I am a prisoner now in my beloved Ham House, and I will never leave.' She died in 1698, an embittered woman.

The ground-floor room to which she retreated, crippled jointly by infirmity and debt, is known as the Duchess's Bedchamber. Highly ornate in decoration and strangely oppressive in atmosphere, the room emits sounds of footsteps and wafts of rose scent at all hours of the day and night. Rose was popular with the Stuart court, both as an effective perfume for the person, and to camouflage less pleasant odours. An exquisite portrait, by Sir Peter Lely, of the Duchess as a young woman hangs over the mantelpiece – but it is the freestanding looking glass to one side which seems to provoke the most shudders. Visitors record a sensation of dread as they peer at the slightly clouded surface, as though they might see in the reflection a face not their own, or catch a glimpse of some malevolent-looking figure standing directly behind them. And household pets are reluctant to enter, standing on the threshold quivering in apparent terror, or spitting and hissing at the portrait. So powerful is the atmosphere in this room that some of the staff take the precaution of deferentially murmuring 'Good afternoon, your Ladyship' before entering.

'I am a prisoner now in my beloved Ham House, and I will never leave…'

ELIZABETH, DUCHESS OF LAUDERDALE

RIGHT *The exterior of Ham House at night.*

During a recent Ghost Club investigation at Ham House, the group was joined by a direct descendant of the Duchess. Using dowsing rods, they were able to establish contact with the ghost, though she would only communicate with her relative. Having correctly identified him as a family member, the Duchess confirmed various facts about the intervening ten generations. She volunteered the information that he had a brother, that his father's life had been unhappy, and that the men of the family traditionally went into the Guards. The entity also claimed that there was a picture of her in the room and, when asked to do so, directed the dowsing rods to the Lely portrait of the Duchess as a young woman, hanging over the fireplace.

The atmosphere in the nearby Dining Room is quite different, but it too is the source of some inexplicable sensations. Elizabeth's second husband was very fond of both convivial company at the dining table, and distinctively aromatic Virginia tobacco. What is perhaps surprising is that certain visitors seem to immediately pick up, not just a scent of tobacco, but a real draught of it. The Mayor of Richmond on a recent visit remarked on it, even though the Mayoress standing next to him could smell nothing. On another occasion, a group of local firemen protested that smoking should not be allowed in a house of this age.

More alarming than scents and perfumes is the accompanying sounds of footsteps on the stairs, usually at night, and which appear not to affect the electronic alarms usually activated by any movement or vibration. Interestingly, if the footsteps are heard going in one direction, they can be heard later returning along the same route. Recently, sets of

LEFT The Great Staircase at Ham. Constructed in 1638–9 for William Murray, it was designed as a magnificent prelude to the splendours of the upstairs State Apartments.

naked footprints have appeared overnight, both on the stairs and in the Duchess's Bedchamber. Staff are unable to explain this strange phenomenon – especially as both sets of prints appear to have lifted the varnish from the ancient floorboards, as though the imprint was burnt on in some way.

The guides have also noticed that they have to be careful where they stand on the stairs while giving an introductory talk to visitors – more than one astonished speaker has had the sensation of a blow or a shove between the shoulder-blades if they have had the temerity to stand on the third step. It may be significant that this spot was also the focus of a strange photograph taken at night in November 2003 by a group of psychic investigators – a white 'orb' of light appears on the image, although it was not visible at the time to witnesses. On analysis neither the photographic equipment nor the film used was found to be faulty.

On numerous occasions a woman in a long black dress has been seen slowly descending the staircase, and turning into the Chapel at the bottom. On the death of her second husband, the Duchess spent a week in the Chapel kneeling and praying over his coffin. It was the finding of a handprint on the rail of the Duchess's pew, clearly visible in the light film of dust the morning after workmen had sealed and set the alarms in the Chapel for the night, which disconcerted the staff and volunteers. The lady in black is sometimes seen entering the chapel followed by a chaplain, believed to be the faithful Gilbert Spinks, her husband's secretary and devoted servant.

But perhaps the most frequent ghostly visitor is a small spaniel-like dog, glimpses of which have been recorded frequently over the last two centuries, trotting purposefully along corridors in the house. Typically it appears running ahead of visitors, up the Great Stairs, into the Museum Room and up to a showcase which covers a former doorway, at which point it promptly vanishes. Indignant visitors have protested that they were forced to leave their pets outside, while 'someone else' had been given permission to bring in their King Charles Spaniel. But when they see the famous painting in the gallery they readily identify the dog they saw a few moments ago. In fact, during recent reconstruction work, workmen removed a large sundial from the centre of the Kitchen Garden and underneath discovered the grave of a small dog. The bones are currently on temporary show in the house, below the double portrait of the Duke and Duchess at the height of their power.

A probably apocryphal tale relating to the ghostly Duchess was recorded in 1879. A six-year old girl was staying overnight at Ham House – thought to be the daughter of the butler – and she awoke in the middle of the night to see an old woman scrabbling at a patch of wall near to the fireplace. The little girl screamed, the apparition disappeared, and subsequent investigations are believed to have turned up a secret compartment hidden in the wall where she was scrabbling, and containing old documents which 'proved' that the Duchess had murdered her first husband in order to marry her second. No trace of this 'proof' has reached the public domain, but Elizabeth's contemporaries clearly thought she was capable of anything.

But there are other apparitions from different eras which also occur at Ham. On frosty winter mornings and late at night, a young man has been seen walking along the terrace, hands clasped, apparently deep in thought. He is believed to be John MacFarlane, who came to stay in the house and promptly fell in love with a lady's maid, an unwise choice in the eyes of his high-born family. His love was unrequited – throughout the winter of 1779 he plied her with gifts and asked her to marry him but she refused (the story is that she was already in love with the Head Steward). In desperation,

'She was violent in everything she set about, a violent friend but a still more violent enemy'

BISHOP BURNET

he etched his name and the date, 1780, into the glass of an upstairs window – the fourth from the right on the terrace façade. Unable to bear his rejection any longer, one night he jumped to his death on the terrace, two floors below. Staff and guests at Ham House have since been horrified to hear a blood-curdling scream outside the top-floor window on the anniversary of his suicide, and the sound of sobs from the garden area known as 'The Wilderness'. The scream is believed to be that of the repentant maid – who nevertheless did marry the Head Steward.

A poignant story is attached to the sighting of a twentieth-century ghost in what was then an informal gated East garden, but is now the Cherry Garden. The 9th Earl of Dysart had no children of his own, but he was a good uncle to various nephews and nieces, including Leon Sextus Tollemache, who as a child was especially fond of playing in the East Garden. It was at Ham that Leon's uncle threw a special dinner party for the young man, so that he could propose marriage to his girlfriend, who accepted. So the house – and particularly that part of the garden – always had happy associations for Leon.

During the First World War, Leon and many younger male members of the Ham staff were away fighting in France. On the morning of 20 February 1917, the old gardener was startled to see Leon, wearing full army uniform, in the garden. He hurried to the main house, expecting to be the first with the surprising news that the young master had been sent home on leave from the Front, where he was serving as an officer, but the gardener was told he must have been mistaken.

A few days later the telegram arrived – Leon had been killed in action on the very morning he was seen in his favourite garden.

The 9th Earl was confined to a wheelchair later in his life following a hunting accident, but every Christmas Eve he made a point of leaving the building by the West door. Bearing his weight on a stick, he would slowly walk across the courtyard to the cottage where his chauffeur, Mr Alan, lived with his family, to give them a basket of presents. On the first Christmas Eve after the Earl died in 1935, Mr Alan heard the unmistakable sounds of the West door closing, and through a window saw the familiar figure advancing slowly with stick and basket. There was a double thump on the door of the cottage, but when the bewildered chauffeur opened it, the courtyard was deserted.

The 9th Earl's wheelchair is still to be seen in the house. Staff are mystified to explain how, whenever the chair is moved from its regular spot for cleaning and other domestic routines, it always seems to return to its original place by morning, despite the sensitive alarms which should detect any movement.

One happier vision occasionally seen at Ham House is the figure of an attractive young woman glimpsed at a particular window on the first floor. She wears an ornate, eighteenth-century dress and waves with one hand, keeping the other firmly behind her back. This spirit is believed to be that of Charlotte Walpole, the natural daughter of Edward Walpole and niece of Sir Horace Walpole, the Gothic novelist, Member of Parliament and bon viveur. Charlotte was illegitimate and this gave her dubious social status, but she was wealthy and the 5th Earl Dysart, who had social clout but little money, was fond of her and married her within a week of their first meeting. There was advantage to both sides. As Charlotte put it:

'If I was but 19 I would refuse point blank. I do not like to be married in a week to a man I never saw. But I am two and twenty. Some people say I am handsome, some say I am not. I believe the truth is that I am likely to be large and go off soon. It is dangerous to refuse so great a match.'

An appealing portrait of Charlotte can be seen in the Great Hall. One hand is concealed in the painting – it is believed that she had a withered or deformed hand. When Charlotte appears nowadays, it is usually seen as a presentiment of something good happening to the present-day residents and staff at Ham, such as a recovery from illness, or the safe delivery of a baby. Perhaps, therefore, it is fitting that Charlotte's illustrious uncle was one of the many visitors over the centuries to surmise that Ham House has many ghostly inhabitants.

'Every minute I expected to see ghosts sweeping by; ghosts I would not give sixpence to see, Lauderdales, Tallemaches (sic) and Maitlands…'
SIR HORACE WALPOLE

HANBURY HALL, WORCESTERSHIRE

Less than three miles from Droitwich is this pretty red-brick William and Mary style house dating from 1701. Hanbury Hall is the quintessential country squire's residence, known for its delicately painted ceilings and staircase, its Orangery, ice-house and pavilions, and delightful eighteenth-century garden and surrounding parkland. But the apparent order and control visible in this perfect estate is belied by the ghost story associated with it, a tale of urgent passions, hidden identities and lost and restored fortunes, worthy of a Restoration comedy.

Emma Vernon was a society beauty, and heiress to Hanbury Hall. In 1778 she married Henry Cecil, heir to the Earldom of Exeter. The marriage was not a success, because in spite of their extensive fortunes they fell into debt and became disenchanted with each other. By 1789, Emma had fallen passionately in love with the local curate, William Sneyd. Emma and William caused a great scandal by eloping together, flying in the face of social mores. It wasn't so much that she was having an affair, it was the fact that she was prepared to overturn social convention by falling in love with a man so much her social inferior, and to risk losing not only her reputation but her considerable fortune, that caused the most censure in high society.

Henry Cecil was shocked to the core by the scandal, and deeply in debt – he fled from Hanbury to a Shropshire farm, adopted the pseudonym of John Jones, and soon found himself embroiled with the farmer's daughter Sarah Hoggins, also known as Sally. Forced to marry, virtually at gunpoint, Henry took the path of least resistance, secretly divorcing Emma (which allowed her to marry her curate) and remarrying Sally, who had no idea of her husband's true identity. But in 1793 Henry inherited the title of Lord Exeter and the Cecil family seat at Burghley. The unwitting Sally was promptly transported from modest surroundings in Shropshire to a vast country house in Lincolnshire, where the servants called her 'my Lady'. The tale of the 'Cottage Countess', as she became known, was delightfully recounted by Tennyson in his poem, 'The Lord of Burghley'.

But the tale did not have a happy ending for all those involved. It is Emma's ghost which is now said to wander her beloved Hanbury Hall and its grounds, and there have been a number of reported sightings, especially along Church Avenue (Emma would walk from the Hall to the church where William had been the curate). One evening, a woman, who was a stranger to the area, was driving home after visiting her brother who lived in the neighbourhood. Her route took her through Hanbury Woods, where she suddenly spotted a young woman, dressed all in black, standing motionless at the side of the road. Concerned that it might not be safe for the girl to be making her way home on foot in such a deserted spot, the driver stopped – only to find that the girl had vanished. Puzzled, she drove on and put the experience to the back of her mind. It was only months later, when her brother mentioned the ghost of Emma Vernon that the lady motorist realised who – or what – she had seen that night.

'...So peaceful rests, without a stone, a name,
What once had beauty, titles, wealth and fame.
How loved, how honour'd once, avails thee not,
To whom related, or by whom begot;
A heap of dust alone remains of thee,
'Tis all thou art, and all the proud shall be!'

ALEXANDER POPE, 'ELEGY TO THE MEMORY OF AN UNFORTUNATE LADY'

RIGHT The South Front of Hanbury Hall, formerly home to the loveless couple Henry Cecil and Emma Vernon.

HIGH PEAK ESTATE, DERBYSHIRE

The famous Winnat's Pass on the High Peak was originally known as 'Wyndegates', which means the pass through which the wind sweeps. This spectacular limestone gorge is a bleak spot at night, and is believed to be haunted by the ghosts of a young couple, Clara and Henry, who were murdered there in 1758. They had eloped to be married at the church in the Peak Forest, but they stopped at an inn to allow their horses to rest. Here they were spotted by a group of lead-miners, who assumed that such a well-dressed young couple would be carrying valuables. So they ambushed Henry and Clara in Winnats Gorge later that night, took their possessions, murdered them and buried their bodies near a barn close by.

The murderers were never positively identified or convicted, though local legend has it that they each died violently – one went mad, another hanged himself and the third was crushed to death by a rock-fall. Decades later, the skeletons of the two young lovers were discovered by miners working in Winnat's Pass, and the remains were buried in Castleton churchyard. Even today some local people believe that on windy nights the ghosts of the murdered lovers can be heard begging for mercy in Winnat's Pass.

The village of Edale at the start of the Pennine Way used to be a remote hamlet, often cut off by heavy snowfall for days or even weeks in winter. During the Middle Ages, packs of wolves roamed the area, and in more recent times there have been sightings of a huge, phantom black dog near Upper Booth, especially on The Tips, the heaps of excavated stones and earth thrown up during the construction of a railway tunnel. In the 1920s newspaper reports told how the area was being terrorised by a huge black dog, which was capable of slaughtering and mutilating dozens of sheep in the course of a single night. A few years later a huge dog was seen close-up by a local girl, but as it passed her it seemed to drift straight through a wire fence – and instantly disappeared.

The highest mountain in the Peak District is Kinder Scout, a wild expanse of moorland and exposed rock formations. There are tales of a water spirit who inhabits a strange expanse of water below Kinder Downfall. The Mermaid's Pool is an eerie stretch of black marshy water. It is said that no fish can survive in it and no animal will drink from it. The water spirit is believed to be visible in the water on Easter eve, and anyone who sees it will either be granted immortality or else be dragged into the water and drowned.

The 'Kinder Boggart' was once said to roam the Downfall, terrifying farmers and shepherds in this remote area. A 'boggart' is an archaic word for a spectre or ghost, related to the better-known term 'bogeyman', and probably originally derived from the Welsh word for ghost, 'bo'. At South Head Farm the graphic sounds of a brutal murder are sometimes re-enacted; even the sound of the victim's body being dragged downstairs can be heard. A nearby meadow is believed to be haunted by the ghost of a lady in white. In the early twentieth century an group of itinerant Irish farm-workers were adamant that they saw a 'girl in white' drift down across the field to the stream, to the spot where the murdered woman's body had been dumped. Having just arrived in the locale, they had no knowledge of the story of the boggart.

'…even today some local people believe that on windy nights the ghosts of the murdered lovers can be heard begging for mercy in Winnat's Pass…'

HINTON AMPNER, HAMPSHIRE

'I was still very unwilling to report these occurrences; although I had taken every means of investigating them I could not discover the least appearance of a trick. On the contrary I was convinced that the noises were beyond the power of any mortal agent....'

MRS MARY RICKETTS,
MANUSCRIPT DATED JULY 1772

Old Hinton Ampner house was considered at one time to be the most haunted house in England. In fact, so chillingly horrible were its ghostly manifestations that the original Tudor house was demolished in 1793, and only the kitchen gardens and part of the stables survive to the present day.

The well-appointed Tudor manor house became the property of Edward, 4th Lord Stawell, and his wife Mary. They lived at Hinton Ampner with Mary's younger sister, Honoria, who died there in 1754. Edward died the following year, of 'apoplexy', but both he and his sister-in-law were to achieve posthumous fame and a certain amount of notoriety when in 1765 Hinton was let to the Ricketts family.

Almost immediately Mr and Mrs Ricketts found that there was 'something curious, something inexplicable about the house'. He was abroad for much of the time, as he had property in Jamaica, but she subsequently wrote a detailed and fascinating account of her experiences. Her tale began with 'noises in the night, as of people shutting, or slamming, doors,' documented the appearance to servants of a man in drab-coloured clothes, and a lady in a dark silk dress, and went on to describe 'the most dismal groans and rustling around [her] bed'. The entire household's night-time slumbers were rent with a cacophony of chilling shrieks, hideous groans, muffled conversations, running footsteps and banging doors.

By 1770, Mrs Ricketts' health was suffering – the couple could not retain servants and if anything the nocturnal manifestations seemed to be increasing in intensity. Mrs Ricketts' brother, the redoubtable Admiral Jervis, sat up all night with the dual comfort of a friend, Captain Luttrell, and a brace of pistols, determined to establish the truth. Within an hour there was a great commotion, the usual sounds of banging doors and running footsteps. 'They immediately rushed out of their respective rooms, pistols in hand, to find nothing except each other', wrote Mrs Ricketts. After a further week of nocturnal vigils, in which, if anything, the phenomena appeared to grow more severe, the baffled and sleep-starved Admiral removed his sister and her family to Winchester and the haunted house was left empty.

But the mystery did not end there. A strange find was reported and appeared as an extract in *Lord Halifax's Ghost Book*, first published in 1936:

'The house was never again occupied and since its reputation was such that tenants were unobtainable, it was at last decided to pull it down [in 1793]. During the work of demolition the workmen found under the floor of one of the rooms a small skull said to be that of a monkey. It was in a box, and close by were a number of papers which had apparently been hidden under the floor of the hall during the Civil War.'

This was taken as proof of a disturbing story which had long circulated in the neighbourhood, that the ghosts were those of Edward, Lord Stawell, and his sister-in-law, Honoria Stewkeley, and that they had done away with a child they had produced, and concealed its remains under the floorboards.

The old manor house was replaced by a Victorian house, which then was subsequently altered, then burnt down and rebuilt again some fifty metres south of the site of the Tudor property. The present house is apparently not troubled by ghostly manifestations, but ardent ghost hunters have reported sensations of great unease in the area where the original building stood.

'…one staff member had the unnerving experience of seeing the figure of Disraeli in the corner of his office…it was just a momentary glimpse but the effect was profound, filling him with a sense of 'cold dread'…'

HUGHENDEN MANOR, BUCKINGHAMSHIRE

Most spirits can be difficult to identify, but there is no mistaking the distinctively dandyish appearance of Benjamin Disraeli. The statesmen, novelist and wit was elevated to the peerage by Queen Victoria as Earl of Beaconsfield, and he remained her favourite prime minister throughout his life. The originator of that telling phrase, 'the greasy pole', acquired Hughenden Manor in 1848 while temporarily out of political favour, and lived there till his death in 1881. 'Dizzy' and his wife Mary Anne adored Hughenden, constantly making improvements to convert a reasonably modest, plain Georgian manor house into a colourful and comfortable mid-Victorian house at the heart of a grand estate with an arboretum and spectacular views.

There have been a number of accounts of strange experiences at Hughenden. One of the small rooms upstairs, when closed up at the end of the day, tends to exude a mysterious 'old-fashioned perfume', for no obvious reason. Many people have remarked on it, though some seem unable to perceive it at all.

The house has been rebuilt many times on the same site, growing in status each time, 'from hovel, to hut, to house,' as one expert memorably puts it. The lowest parts of the present building incorporate the remains of a medieval house – there is even a window dating from the late Middle Ages on one of the staircases. Robert Blake, Disraeli's biographer, researched his famous book in the strong room of the basement and apparently reported several sightings of a man in archaic clothes walking straight through the basement.

One staff member had the unnerving experience of seeing the figure of Disraeli in the corner of his office, which used to be the Smoking Room in the premier's time. It was a September day. As the member of staff re-entered his office he was shocked to see a dandyish figure dressed in black, with a walking stick, standing half-turned towards him, next to the filing cabinet. It was just a momentary glimpse but the effect was profound, filling him with a sense of 'cold dread'. He is adamant that it could not have been a trick of the light, but was reluctant to mention it to colleagues for fear of ridicule. Three months later, a fellow employee casually told him that those upstairs rooms were known to be haunted. He has also reported the sensation, on several occasions, that a large number of people were gradually filling up the otherwise empty dining room downstairs, though there was nothing to be seen.

On numerous occasions Dizzy has been glimpsed by visitors near the portrait at the foot of the stairs. People assume he is an actor in historical costume, or one of the house staff impersonating the former premier, only to realise that the figure has 'dissolved'.

Unlike the rest of the house, the Library has an atmosphere which some people find slightly depressing. It used to be the Drawing Room, and this was where Disraeli's coffin lay in state after his death in London in 1881. When a staff member sat in the chair at the desk to write a routine note, he had the distinct sensation of having committed 'an impertinence' and got up again very quickly. On occasions, people have sensed a presence sitting at the desk in the Study when the house is otherwise empty.

The apparitions at Hughenden are rarely eerie, however. The house has a good atmosphere, and everything is on a very domestic scale, and quite homely. Disraeli and his wife loved the place, and it is possible that such strong personalities would imprint themselves on susceptible visitors.

'…The first night she spent there, her watch stopped dead at midnight – so the next day she replaced the battery, and the watch worked as normal until midnight the next night, when once again it stopped…'

KING'S HEAD,
AYLESBURY, BUCKINGHAMSHIRE

A very ancient coaching inn, The King's Head dates from around 1450. The oldest pub in Aylesbury, it is reputed to be thoroughly haunted.

The current Custodian spent six months living on site in the staff accommodation when she was first appointed, and for the first few nights slept in the Cromwell Room (so called because it was believed that Cromwell stayed there, though this has since been found to be untrue.) The room has a distinct atmosphere, and no-one is inclined to sleep there; it seems somehow menacing and unnerving, with dark-coloured, wide wooden floorboards with a pronounced slope. The Custodian was initially sceptical but subsequently felt sure there was 'definitely a presence' in the Cromwell Room; subsequent investigations by members of the Ghost Club apparently picked up the spirit of a 'mad, cackling woman' in that room.

The first night she spent there, her watch stopped dead at midnight – so the next day she replaced the battery, and the watch worked as normal until midnight the next night, when once again it stopped. Although she was normally a heavy sleeper, she kept waking up throughout the night, sitting bolt upright numerous times, but unable to identify what had woken her so suddenly. She moved into another bedroom, and felt more at ease in the building, but a few months later another colleague stayed in the Cromwell Room – and his watch also stopped dead on midnight.

A nocturnal investigation at the pub by the Ghost Club in April 2004 was full of incident, with subsequent accounts of many ghosts in residence, including an apparent sighting of a Catholic priest, a Victorian child, and a servant from the 1550s who had died in a fire. The Custodian's predecessor would occasionally catch sight of the figure of a man at the top of the cellar steps, as well as the ghost of a man believed to be Oliver Cromwell; the last sighting was on the day of the funeral of the Queen Elizabeth the Queen Mother.

LANHYDROCK, CORNWALL

Originally the site belonged to the Bodmin-based Priory of St Petroc, until the Dissolution of the Monasteries in 1536–40. The house was completed by the Robartes family in the seventeenth century and to this day Lanhydrock seems to exude an air of serenity. But in 1881 the house was damaged by a fire which began in the kitchen roof. The conflagration took hold so quickly that Lady Robartes, aged 68, had to be rescued by a ladder from an upstairs window. The shock was too great for her and she died a few days later. Lord Robartes never recovered from the loss of his wife and home, and died the next year. Their son, Thomas, immediately had the house refurbished in the Jacobean style. He used the latest advances in Victorian technology and planning, but followed the basic outer form of the original building.

The largely late-Victorian house has long had a reputation for being haunted by an impressive variety of ghosts. A dapper gent wearing Victorian clothes complete with a top hat is frequently glimpsed, there is a grey lady, and a man supposedly hanged outside the Gatehouse by the Royalist army in the seventeenth century. In addition there are accounts of sudden whiffs of cigar smoke and the sounds of children's laughter in other rooms.

Paul Holden, the current House and Collections Manager at Lanhydrock, was involved in a fascinating investigation which took place in June 2004, when ten members of the Paranormal Research Organisation held a night-time vigil in four of the most 'active' sites within the house. These were the Long Gallery, the Nursery Suite, the male and female servants' quarters, and the Prayer Room and Prayer Room Corridor. Their accounts of the ghosts they encountered in a single evening include a maidservant who had died after falling downstairs in the 1820s; a toddler who apparently perished from scarlet fever at about the same time; a 10-year-old girl called Emily who died of a heart problem in the 1760s; a former head butler called Albert Leah who succumbed to natural causes around 1890; a teenage boy who had been trampled to death by a horse in 1795; an Irish servant called Annabelle O'Connor who committed suicide at the age of 22 because she was pregnant by a fellow servant who was already married; a small boy called Robert who liked to play hide and seek in the Luggage Room; a cheerful tailor who also cleaned the household's shoes; a dapper gent with top hat and blue waistcoat; and a sixteenth-century Catholic priest wracked with guilt over his affair with a female domestic and the baby son subsequently born to her.

In addition, the investigators recorded a number of measurable but inexplicable physical phenomena, such as sudden drops in temperature, the sudden smell of a strong perfume, an astonishingly dense sense of darkness and the misbehaviour of otherwise reliable camera equipment, and the subsequent appearance of 'orbs' on photographic film once developed. One group also reported seeing lights moving around a book in the Long Gallery – it was the *Brevium Romanum*, a book of Latin prayers and readings published in 1568.

'Even the most sceptical of NT staff who were accompanying the investigators were struck by the abnormalities that were observed…there was some movement of inanimate objects such as coins, shadows seen moving on the Teak Stairs, violently fluctuating EMF (Electromagnetic field) readings, observed orbs in several areas, a light in the servants' passage inexplicably going out, and unexplained noises in the Long Gallery,' said Paul.

So striking is the level of ghostly activity at Lanhydrock that even those who left there long ago remember their

'One of the most common questions asked by our visitors has always been, "Have you got any ghosts?" Well, some of our staff have certainly reported seeing or feeling a presence of sorts….'

PAUL HOLDEN, HOUSE AND COLLECTIONS MANAGER

experiences vividly. Joyce Rowe was a housemaid at Lanhydrock between 1940 and 1945. Her daily routine was tough, rising at 4.30am and starting work at 5am. She spent most of every day on her hands and knees, scrubbing and cleaning floors. As the war progressed, nearly all the other domestic staff left to devote themselves to the war effort and soon only Joyce and the Head Housemaid were left. Her sleeping quarters were moved to a smaller room at the top of the house but she could only sleep there once before refusing to ever spend the night in the room again. She described how she had been sitting up in bed at around 11:30pm, reading a book of hymns, when suddenly she felt the room temperature plummet. And then, 'I had the awful feeling of someone pressing down on me'. Too terrified to move, she sat awake all night. The next morning she described her terrors to Eve the Head Housemaid who confessed that, 'We put you in there knowing you didn't know anything about it – we've known it's been haunted for years.'

Later, Joyce was told that a former Lord Robartes had been an inveterate gambler and, half in jest, one night offered his daughter in marriage as his stake in a card game. Rather than marry the gentleman who had 'won' her, the daughter committed suicide by jumping from the tower – and the little room in which Joyce had tried to sleep had been her bedroom.

This explanation for this story is, however, unlikely, as the room in question is part of the Victorian servants' quarters. None of the Robartes family gambled a daughter, and only a boy, Alexander Agar-Robartes, committed suicide between the wars. This room would never have been a high-status bedroom. But perhaps this convoluted and romantic story has humbler origins, in the apparent suicide of 22-year old Annabelle O'Connor, the pregnant Irish servant encountered during the Paranormal Research Organisation's vigil?

Recently Joyce Rowe returned to Lanhydrock with friends, and out of curiosity they climbed to the long corridor from which the bedrooms led, including the room which had given her the horrors so many years before. Sunlight was streaming into the landing, and the doors were warm to the touch – all except the one giving onto the haunted bedroom, which was 'icy cold'.

'We put you in there knowing you didn't know anything about it – we've known it's been haunted for years.'

HEAD HOUSEMAID TO A JUNIOR IN THE 1940s

LLANERCHAERON, CEREDIGION

A rare survival, Llanerchaeron is an eighteenth-century gentry estate near the west coast of Wales, which has survived virtually intact into the twenty-first century. It was designed and built by John Nash in 1794–6 and is the most complete example of his early work in existence. The estate was designed to be largely self-sufficient – as well as the attractive house and surrounding parkland there is a dairy, laundry, brewery and salting house, and the buildings of the garden and Home Farm.

In its heyday, the house and estate would have been a bustling, lively place, full of everyday activity and the comings and goings of servants and the family. There is still a sense at Llanerchaeron that this is a very 'lived-in' property. Since the estate opened to the public, staff and volunteers have been aware of occasional glimpses of former occupants, a sensation of being watched, or of seeing something flitting past just beyond the field of vision. A figure has been seen standing in the Inner Hall – mysteriously disappearing as soon as a member of staff turns to look more closely – and some have heard footsteps approaching them from behind, and turned round to find no-one there.

Objects at Llanerchaeron seem to have a tendency to move of their own volition – a coal scuttle once moved from its customary place by the fireplace into the middle of the Dining Room – only the Room Steward had been in the room at the time, and he was adamant he hadn't touched it. Similarly, the window behind the steward's chair in this room has been known to shake violently, as though there were a gale outside, or someone was desperately trying to get in.

The Upstairs Meeting Room harbours some particularly mysterious goings-on. This room was once a bedroom and

ABOVE *The dark, claustrophobic cellar at Llanerchaeron.*

the lights often switch themselves on, despite the door being securely locked. On occasions, staff feel that someone is leaning against the door from the other side to prevent entry, but the force gives in when met by a polite knock. Footsteps are often heard coming from the Upstairs Meeting Room by those in the room below.

It is evident that Llanerchaeron's domestic quarters have a less welcoming atmosphere than the rest of the house. One night a member of staff was working late, measuring the Housekeeper's Room (now an office), when suddenly the door slammed shut on him with a terrific bang, and was stuck fast. The house was completely empty at the time, so no-one could have shut him in as a joke, and there were bars on the windows so there was no way out. Eventually he managed to break a panel on the door and escape.

In the Bell Corridor, before the house was taken over and restored by the National Trust, there was an old electric light from which a freezing fog seemed to seep. Even on bright sunny days there is still an icy chill palpable beneath this light. And in the kitchen, the Welsh dresser occasionally rattles violently as though it is being shaken by an unseen force. 'Perhaps it's the ghost of the cook, angry at the way her kitchen has been overrun!' comments the Property Manager.

'…On occasions, staff feel that someone is leaning against the door from the other side to prevent entry, but the force gives in when met by a polite knock…'

93

LEFT Lodge Park, the creation and home of John 'Crump' Dutton.

'…Betty Hall, former housekeeper to Charles Dutton, the 7th Lord Sherborne, would often hear 'Crump's impatient footsteps pounding up and down a wooden staircase — but when she examined the spot from which she heard the footsteps, there was nothing but fresh air…'

LODGE PARK AND SHERBORNE ESTATE, GLOUCESTERSHIRE

The Sherborne Estate encompasses 1,650 hectares (4,000 acres) of rolling Cotswold countryside, with glorious views down to the River Windrush. At the heart lies Lodge Park, now a house but originally a grandstand for deer coursing and a banqueting house.

Lodge Park was the brainchild of one man, and it grew from his dual passions for gambling and banqueting. John 'Crump' Dutton, Member of Parliament and Deputy Lieutenant for Gloucestershire, was a larger-than-life character, so much so that he is believed by some to still reside at Lodge Park, which he created in 1634.

On his memorial in Sherborne Church, 'Crump' is remembered as 'One who was Master of a large Fortune and Owner of a Mind Equal to it'. Betty Hall, former housekeeper to Charles Dutton, the 7th Lord Sherborne, would often hear 'Crump's impatient footsteps pounding up and down a wooden staircase — but when she examined the spot from which she heard the footsteps, there was nothing but fresh air. Subsequent research revealed that there had once been a set of wooden stairs located at that spot, but they had been removed in the late seventeenth century, some time after 'Crump' had been living there. Betty was convinced that he was still haunting Lodge Park, and would respectfully set a place for him at the dinner table.

Perhaps there is a certain irony that John Dutton, a man who so loved gambling, should come to an untimely end as the result of an accident caused by a high-spirited horse. Accounts vary, but it seems he was either thrown from his horse in Larkethill Wood, or knocked down by his own horse and carriage when he was attempting to open a gate on the estate. He died at Lodge Park as a result of his injuries in 1656.

'Crump' was a popular figure in the area and his memory lives on today amongst the dart-playing regulars at the Sherborne Arms in Aldsworth. When they throw a bad shot, tradition dictates they shout 'Crump Dutton!', an elegant improvement on many better-known imprecations.

LYME PARK, CHESHIRE

Opulent and impressive, Lyme Park has had a number of incarnations during the 550 years it was owned by the Legh family. It began as a medieval house, famed for its deer-hunting, then underwent a substantial rebuilding in the 1550s at the hands of Sir Piers Legh, who wanted an impressive Tudor mansion. It was his descendant, Peter Legh, who commissioned the final dramatic transformation, making the house into a Palladian palace in the 1720s at the hands of Venetian architect Giacomo Leoni. The interior is now famous for its Mortlake tapestries and Grinling Gibbons wood-carvings. The house itself is an intriguing blend of impressive state rooms and darker, older Elizabethan sections, with wood-panelled chambers and secret passages.

At the heart of the old house is a fine gallery, 35 metres (120 feet) long, where in Tudor times the family and their guests would have taken exercise in inclement weather and entertained themselves indoors. The Gallery leads to the Knight's Bedroom, and these two rooms are the focus of a number of ghost stories associated with Lyme. Low-ceilinged and ornate, and dominated by a four-poster bed, the room has an oppressive atmosphere, so perhaps it is not surprising that visitors have commented on sudden drops in temperature and wafts of unusual smells.

Lyme Park's best-known ghost story is set in the medieval deer park which encircles the house and gardens. For centuries witnesses have given accounts of seeing and hearing a phantom cortège moving slowly though the park to Knight's Low, a small hill. Behind the procession walks a woman in white, known as Blanche. Sir Piers Legh died in Paris in 1422 from wounds he received while fighting the French at the Battle of Meux. He had wanted to be buried at Lyme Park, so his loyal retainers brought his body back to Cheshire and rested on the final homeward stretch at Knight's Low. Sir Piers was married to Lady Joan, but he also had a mistress named Blanche, and it is her ghost which is believed to follow the cortège, wracked with grief.

Interestingly, it seems that over the intervening centuries, the image of the whole cortège has 'faded' with the passage of time, and more recent accounts only mention the distraught figure of Blanche.

'…For centuries witnesses have given accounts of seeing and hearing a phantom cortège moving slowly though the park to Knight's Low, a small hill. Behind the procession walks a woman in white, known as Blanche…'

'…low-ceilinged and ornate, and
dominated by a four-poster bed, the
room has an oppressive atmosphere…'

LYVEDEN NEW BIELD, NORTHAMPTONSHIRE

An incomplete Elizabethan garden house and moated garden in a very isolated part of Northamptonshire, Lyveden New Bield is described even by the staff who work there as 'profoundly spooky'. The building is a melancholy relic, an indirect victim of the Gunpowder Plot of 1605. It was created in 1595 by Sir Thomas Tresham, who wanted to build a remarkable house to symbolise his Catholic faith. His dream was to express his religion in bricks and mortar by constructing a dwelling place which would represent the Passion of Christ. The 'footprint' of the building is in the shape of the Cross.

But ten years later, with the family implicated in the ill-fated plot to blow up King James I and Parliament, and in serious debt, Thomas Tresham died, and all work stopped abruptly. What is left of Lyveden is the skeleton or shell of the grand house that never was – never completed, roofed or glazed. All the more reason for alarm, then, when, two years ago, the current property manager clearly saw a long-faced, bearded man standing at one bay of the upper-storey windows. The figure appeared to walk across the window before disappearing from view. Yet there are no floors inside the shell of Lyveden, so whom – or what – did he see? Intriguingly, a local printer also reported seeing a figure of a similar description at one of the bay windows, 35 feet (7 metres) off the ground. Locals are adamant that it would be impossible for anyone to be suspended at that height or to climb up inside the building, so did they in fact see the shadow of Sir Thomas Tresham, worrying over his builders' lack of progress?

The grounds around the house are also very resonant; recent excavations have established that Lyveden New Bield occupies land which was once a flourishing village. An experiment with dowsing confirmed that two converging ley lines meet at the site and the focus seems to be the East bay of the house itself. In addition, local folklore has it that the Middle Garden (also known as the Moated Garden) is haunted by Scottish ghosts. Ninety-eight men of the 43rd Highland Regiment, the Black Watch, were surrounded by the King's Men in 1743, and surrendered without bloodshed, though one died of hunger and is believed to be buried within the Water Garden. All were court-martialled and sentenced to death; in the event, three were shot while the rest were sent to Georgia or the West Indies, from which few returned alive. According to legend, on stormy nights the pipes and drums of the Black Watch regiment can still be heard.

ABOVE *Silhouette of Lyveden New Bield against the early morning sky. The figure of Sir Thomas Tresham, the building's owner and designer, has been seen in the windows.*

'*...on stormy nights the pipes and drums of the Black Watch regiment can still be heard...*'

MOMPESSON HOUSE, WILTSHIRE

Mompesson House stands just inside the entrance to The Cathedral Close in Salisbury, overlooking Choristers' Green. It was built in 1701 and is considered to be perhaps the best example in England of Queen Anne domestic architecture. It is also linked to a remarkable ghost story affecting members of the Mompesson family.

The house was built by Thomas Mompesson, and completed by his son after his death. Both Thomas and his cousin John had been staunch Royalists who suddenly found themselves in favour and fortune following the Restoration of Charles II. During the Civil War, both men had fought for the King. The war claimed many casualties and took a particularly high toll of drummer boys, often the first in the firing line.

Around 1660, with the war over, John Mompesson was disturbed in his Tedworth home by a peculiar, ragged vagrant who persisted in drumming loudly in the street. Mompesson had the instrument confiscated and its owner put in custody, but this seems to have been an unwise move. The bailiff had the drum delivered to the Mompessons' home – and that's when the trouble began.

On his return home following a trip to London, Mompesson found his wife in a state of considerable anguish, claiming that the house must have been attached by thieves during the night, because of the terrible knocking noises and general commotion. Three nights later the same sounds could be heard, with violent banging emanating from the outer doors and walls – Mr Mompesson loaded his pistols and conducted a detailed search of the premises, but could see nothing amiss. This was the beginning of what was to be three years of disturbances and persecution of the Mompesson family in their Tedworth house.

The Staircase Hall (LEFT) and Library (RIGHT) at Mompesson.

The disturbances were typical of those associated with poltergeist activity, with objects being thrown, children lifted bodily out of their beds. But the most persistent and maddening phenomenon was the incessant beating of the drum, in a recognisable military rhythm, night after night. No explanation could be found, but many witnesses testified to the same experiences. Finally, in 1663, the offending vagrant, William Drury, was arrested and tried at Salisbury for witchcraft, but acquitted.

The Mompesson story has a curious modern postscript. In the 1950s a Mr Hammick, a former occupant of Mompesson House, returned to visit the new owner, Mr Denis Martineau. When he told the story of the drummer boy Mr Martineau produced a brass drummer boy's badge. He had found it under the floor of the room where the drum was thought to have been kept.

'…But the most persistent and maddening phenomenon was the incessant beating of the drum, in a recognisable military rhythm, night after night…'

'…Disembodied voices, echoing footsteps and the soft rustling of unseen fabrics have been reported by witnesses…'

NEWARK PARK, GLOUCESTERSHIRE

Dramatically sited on the edge of a 12-metre (40-foot) limestone cliff, Newark Park is an unusual house with an intriguing history. It was originally built in the 1550s as a Tudor hunting lodge, and this is still evident on the east-facing façade, but in the 1790s the building was remodelled by James Wyatt and given its Georgian Gothic south-facing façade. Surrounded by a landscaped park and woods, Newark has a spectacular location on a spur of the Cotswolds providing inspiring views over the Gloucestershire countryside towards the Mendip hills and Marlborough Downs.

Newark has been inhabited for more than 400 years, and although it has a warm atmosphere, tales abound of its hauntings. The stories are attributed to the very stones of its construction – following the Dissolution of the Monasteries, Sir Nicholas Poyntz acquired Kingswood Abbey, which he demolished to provide the building materials for his 'new work', Newark. Some people believe that this early example of architectural salvage may have backfired; along with the ready-shaped masonry came some of the spirits of the dispossessed monks.

Strange sounds seem to be Newark Park's trademark. Disembodied voices, echoing footsteps and the soft rustling of unseen fabrics have been reported by witnesses. One winter's evening, when the current Custodian was alone in the house, quietly reading in his small sitting room which is in the sixteenth-century part of the building, he was suddenly aware that something or someone had walked across the floor of the room above him. He distinctly heard footsteps. As he knew no-one else was in the house he went upstairs and looked in the room known as the Green Bedroom. Nothing was to be seen but the room had a distinct chill about it. This became a familiar occurrence at Newark – the Green Bedroom is known to be haunted.

On another occasion, the Custodian came downstairs from the second floor to find his Great Dane, Boston, standing on the half-landing at the top of the main staircase. The dog was giving out a slow growl and watching something at the foot of the stairs intensely. 'Boston's fur running down her spine was upright and the more her head moved following whatever it was she could see, the more intense her growl became,' said the Custodian. 'This lasted for all of ten minutes, I could see nothing but something was decidedly upsetting Boston!'

In the late 1980s a photographer was working in the house taking photographs for a magazine article. The photo shoot went smoothly, but a few weeks later, when the photographer sent back one of the pictures he had taken, there was an unexplained blemish on the print. It looked curiously like a figure walking across the room, though no-one else had been in the room when the photograph was taken.

Patches of intense cold and inexplicable lights have also been reported by visitors and locals alike. As the Custodian explains: 'Living in a house that is open to the public provides an opportunity for complete strangers to come up to you and tell you that they have had a strange experience while going around the house. This has happened to me on more than one occasion. Some people say "I just had to get out of that room"; some will tell you that they saw someone in a room when all the time the room was empty; and others will tell you that they had a chill down their spine when in a certain part of the house.'

Nevertheless, the Custodian feels that the atmosphere has lightened since the days of his predecessor, who lived in the house while it was still semi-derelict. 'As the house has come back to life, the restless spirits that inhabit it have become less active,' he says. 'Whatever it is at Newark has always been benign, and not malevolent.'

'...Every night, 'something' came through the wall over her bed...'

NUNNINGTON HALL, YORK

On the banks of the River Rye, in North Yorkshire, is a seventeenth-century manor house with a delightful, sheltered walled garden. Nunnington Hall, with its magnificent oak panelling, three staircases, nursery and family rooms, has long had a reputation for being haunted.

The last tenant of the Hall, Mrs Susan Clive, related how in 1937 a young French lady, Mlle Lilette de Foucauld, came to stay. She was put in the Panelled Room but after a few nights confessed that she had hardly slept because she was terrified. Every night, 'something' came through the wall over her bed – which in those days was against the wall – and went out through the window. She was moved to another bedroom and had no more disturbed nights.

The Proud Lady of Nunnington is believed to haunt the house – she was the second wife of the owner of Nunnington Hall, and bitterly resented her stepson, wishing that her own boy could inherit the estate. In time, the father died, and the stepmother mistreated the older boy, locking him in an attic room. The only person who was allowed to see him was his younger half-brother, who was very fond of him, and would bring him food and toys. One night the older boy escaped – probably with the help of one of the servants – and disappeared without trace. The stepmother was jubilant, but the younger child was distraught – he missed his playmate,

and would watch for him endlessly from the windows. Tragically, he leaned too far out of a window, fell to the ground and died from his injuries. His mother took to roaming the house, inconsolable with grief. After her death, when the property had passed to new owners, there were many reported sightings of her ghost gliding though the rooms and ascending the staircase, accompanied by the sound of rustling from her silk dress.

The top of the staircase is alleged to be haunted by a phantom dog, a family pet that became over-excited and ran along a corridor, jumped through the banisters and fell to its death. Alarmed visitors who were completely unaware of the story have reported the sensation of an invisible dog circling their legs as they peer over the stair rails.

Present-day witnesses have occasionally heard voices, like the sound of a distant party, when they have known the place to be empty. Some have also caught glimpses of a hurrying figure, described as being 'like a flitting shadow'. There is a distinct smell of pipe smoke in the building at times, and local people have reported seeing the ghostly figure of a lady walking down a path in the garden.

'Only a few people haven't heard or seen something at some time,' commented one member of staff. 'It's a very friendly house, yet people do see and experience things they can't explain. But I would happily come into the house late at night – it doesn't have a scary atmosphere.'

ABOVE The Parlour, probably the original kitchen, in the Old Post Office at Tintagel.

THE OLD POST OFFICE, TINTAGEL, CORNWALL

One of the first properties acquired by the National Trust (in 1903) was The Old Post Office in Tintagel, Cornwall. The name Tintagel is known throughout the world in connection with the myths and legends of King Arthur, and the castle is a romantic ruin on a spectacular rocky promontory.

The Old Post Office was a small medieval manor in the heart of the village, weathered and tumbledown. By 1841 the parish of Tintagel was generating more than 120 letters per week, and the village needed its own post office, so the old manor house was pressed into service for the then exciting new form of communication. This building still serves as both house and post office. The roof has gradually subsided under the weight of its slate tiles, and the back wall has been heavily buttressed to help support the weight.

Historic postal and telegraph equipment is located behind the counter, including a Spagnoletti receiver and undulator from the late nineteenth century – an early method of sending messages by what later became known as Morse Code.

Kelly Palmer is the current Custodian of The Old Post Office and has been witness to one particularly ghostly experience. She became aware that every morning when she entered the building the lights would flicker as though in protest at being disturbed, and would continue to flash until just before the building opened each day to visitors. When a visitor reported seeing an old lady in the bed, Kelly decided to use the Spagnoletti receiver to monitor the flashes, to discover that they repeatedly spelt out the words 'Nora' or 'Noah'. So she was not surprised to discover subsequently that a previous resident of the Old Post Office was an elderly lady called Mrs Noah...

POWIS CASTLE, POWYS

It would be surprising if a place as ancient as Powis Castle did not harbour some ghost stories. Powis was the forbidding fortress of a dynasty of Welsh princes in the thirteenth century, was besieged in the fourteenth and fifteenth centuries and attacked and seized by Parliamentary forces during the Civil War. Though the exterior of the castle has changed little since the early Middle Ages, it is now surrounded by magnificent terraced gardens in the baroque style and the interiors and contents are a tribute to the wealth and taste of generations of the Herbert family.

People who work at Powis testify to its 'friendly, homely atmosphere' and yet find it difficult to discount well-recorded stories of ghostly activity over the centuries. Unexplained recent sightings include a woman wearing a mob-cap who appeared to both an administrator and then his son in one of the rooms used for staff accommodation on site. Most recently, the same figure has materialised sitting on the end of the bed of the building supervisor and his wife in their flat in the Ballroom Wing. A less benign manifestation is the sound of a large dog apparently trying vigorously to break out of the old kitchen. Present-day pets tend to give this area a wide berth.

The Duke's Room is located on the cross gallery at the end of the Long Gallery and this area is one of the most haunted in the castle. There have been numerous sightings by staff of fleeting figures in this part of the castle. Members of the public have also have found the area to be strangely crowded – two of them enquired (separately, but on the same day) after the lady in black seen sitting in a chair beside the fireplace, while on another occasion a visitor reported the alarming sensation of the touch of an invisible hand on her arm. Similarly, the house steward spotted a lady standing by the door to the Duke's Room one day, and thought she had imagined it, but later that same day a visitor reported having felt the presence of a woman in the exact same spot.

Most of the after-hours activity at Powis seems to focus on the Ballroom Wing. A magnificent grand piano graces the long, narrow eighteenth-century ballroom, and staff have heard the haunting sounds of piano music when they know the room to be empty and locked. On one occasion the House Manager and a conservator went to the Ballroom together to speak to the piano tuner, whom they believed to be working there. As they climbed the stairs they clearly heard the piano being played but when they entered the room the piano was silent and no-one was in the room.

During recent redecoration work, the piano was laboriously moved from its normal position, only to be discovered back in its original location the following morning, despite the fact that the security alarms should have been triggered by any movement. There are also many accounts of the sound of someone trying to enter or leave by the Ballroom doors – again, when it is impossible that this could be caused by human agency.

Even sceptics have been spooked by the strange atmosphere in the Ballroom. On one occasion a builder descending the stairs into the room in broad daylight suddenly had the impression of a pair of hands being clamped to his shoulders, yet he was entirely alone. Perhaps this sensation was evoked by the sight of the vicious mantraps displayed on the wall at the foot of the staircase. Or perhaps he was picking up the memory of some unfortunate eighteenth-century poacher, apprehended and frog-marched to justice?

ABOVE *Medusa's head screams out of the statue of Fame and Pegasus (c. 1705) by Andries Carpentiere.*

'…a visitor reported the alarming sensation of the touch of an invisible hand on her arm…'

'…the Duke's Room is located on the cross gallery at the end of the Long Gallery and this area is one of the most haunted in the castle…'

RIGHT A view down the Long Gallery at Powis Castle. The hall leads to the Duke's Room – one of the most haunted areas.

LEFT The rear of Quarry Bank Mill, which stands by the side of the River Bollin.

QUARRY BANK MILL, CHESHIRE

Quarry Bank Mill and Styal Estate is the oldest commercial working mill to be spinning and weaving cotton currently operating in Britain. It is also home to Europe's most powerful working waterwheel, and two steam-powered engines. The Styal Estate consists of the factory village of Styal, former home of mill workers and their families, together with areas of riverside, farmland and woodland in the valley of the River Bollin.

The Apprentice House at Quarry Bank was where pauper children were boarded while they were indentured to the Mill. The House was built in 1790 and was home to approximately 90 children at any one time, until 1847. Different Superintendents ran the establishment throughout that period, notably the Shawcrosses and after them the Timperlys. The household also employed skivvies – female servants – to cook and clean. The Apprentice House appears to have some resident ghosts, all of them adult women.

The attics of the Apprentice House seem to be particularly prone to ghostly encounters. Many people remark on a cold spot as they walk down the stairs from the end attic into the medical room and the boys' dormitory. When workmen were renovating the house in the 1980s they claimed to have seen the image of a woman in the end attic while working in the medical room. On another occasion, a staff member was walking round the house, locking up, accompanied by her dog. When they reached the stairs leading to the attics the dog refused to go further and its hackles went up. And the dog would not enter the house at all after this experience.

Visitors with psychic abilities have strong reactions to the attics. One visitor brought a pendulum on the visit which stayed perfectly still until the party reached the end attic, when it began to move violently. Others claim to have seen an apparition of a woman in the attic, once directly behind a house interpreter. One staff member who was totally sceptical about the paranormal swears that as she was closing the doors at dusk, she felt a presence behind her in the end attic.

In the Schoolroom, people have sensed something near the fireplace, and had the sensation that they were being watched. One visitor refused point-blank to enter the Schoolroom, claiming that the house had an evil presence.

The current Custodian and his family live in the cottage attached to the House. Two of their children say that when they were young, they would see 'a lady in old clothes' standing at the bottom of their beds.

At the Mill itself, staff have witnessed the apparition of a woman roaming the top floors. Although the records of fatalities and deadly accidents in the Mill have been consulted, none of them appear to have involved women, so it is not known who this female figure may be, or why she haunts the site.

There's a figure against the moon,
Nobody sees it but I, and it makes my breast beat out of tune ...

THOMAS HARDY, 'WESSEX HEIGHTS', 1896

RHOSSILI, GOWER

The sweeping curve of Rhossili Bay is one of the most beautiful sights in Wales, offset at one end by the strangely zoomorphic shape of Worm's Head. The whole area is rich in ghost stories, and it certainly has a romantic atmosphere, especially in winter. The hinterland, Rhossili Down, was the site of a pre-Norman village, and traces of medieval smallholdings and farming methods can still be seen at the Vile, while the remains of a small, ancient church were excavated recently.

Close to the windswept and lonely beach lies an old rectory, built in 1850 on the site of a much older farmhouse. Dylan Thomas found the place and its location so appealing he wanted to move into it, but the considerable distance to the nearest pub settled the issue, and instead he made his home further north at the Boathouse in Laugharne.

The reason for the lonely location of the rectory is that it was equidistant between two parishes, Llangennith and Rhossili, each lying at opposite ends of the bay. The longest-serving vicar to live here was the Reverend John Ponsonby Lucas, who was based at the rectory from 1855 to 1898. In order to reach his far-flung parishioners, the dedicated and energetic Reverend would mount his powerful horse, and it is believed locally that his ghost can be seen on horseback, galloping along the curve of the beach.

Particularly wild nights summon up the tale of Squire Mansell, dating from 1800, and the ghostly coach-and-four which was driven across the beach by the ghost of the rapacious squire. Squire Mansell had heard that a cache of gold had been uncovered on Rhossili Beach by an unusually low tide, so he raced to the beach in his coach, drove off the villagers who were already at the scene and claimed the majority of the booty for himself. The squire later traced all the villagers he had spotted at the site, and confiscated any gold they had been lucky enough to acquire. He left the area promptly to spend his loot, but when the money ran out several years later he returned to Rhossili and continued to search – fruitlessly – for yet more gold. Some people believe that his coach, drawn by four horses, can be seen on the sands on stormy nights.

'…ghosts include the mischievous, sociable and highly inquisitive GBS himself, the redoubtable Mrs Shaw, and Lawrence of Arabia…'

SHAW'S CORNER, HERTFORDSHIRE

For 46 years, this Edwardian Arts and Crafts-influenced red-brick house in the tiny village of Ayot St Lawrence in Hertfordshire was home to of one of the most prolific and remarkable men of English literature. The Irish-born playwright, philosopher and 'gigantic phenomenon', George Bernard Shaw, chose the house on the unorthodox basis that the locals were reputed to survive to a venerable age. Certainly he proved his own theory by surviving to the advanced age of 94, and his ashes and those of Mrs Shaw are scattered in the garden, near the revolving summerhouse in which he composed some of his greatest plays on sunny days.

The house and its contents remain almost exactly as Shaw left them on the day of his death, 2 November 1950. There is a palpable sense of this mighty individual and the house is brimful of his considerable personality and passions, from his wire-rimmed spectacles to his membership card for the Cyclists Touring Club, dated 1950, when he was nearing his end. The collection of hats, the Rodin bust of the world-famous author, the long woollen underwear, the walking sticks and the alarming hairy tweed suits sit in happy domestic harmony with his Oscar and his pre-printed postcards which were used to answer almost any written query. Photographs of those he admired jostle for pride of place, from his beloved wife Charlotte to those three icons of the early twentieth century, Stalin, Chaplin and Gandhi.

Some staff and volunteers believe the house to be haunted, and successive members of staff living on site have reported a sensation of the house being 'inhabited' even when it is closed to the public. Ghosts include the mischievous, sociable and highly inquisitive GBS himself, the redoubtable Mrs Shaw, and Lawrence of Arabia, who had been a frequent and much-loved visitor.

Paul Williamson, the current Custodian, experienced a number of odd but benign occurrences during his first few months of working at the property. He would return to rooms to find wide-open doors which he knew he had closed up and, on one occasion, three notes sounded a chord on the Bechstein piano in front of Paul and a couple of witnesses, when no-one was near the instrument. On Paul's very first night at the house, the security alarm sounded. This was not in itself unusual, but the same thing had happened to the two previous locums on their first nights there too.

There is a story which was recounted in the Herts Advertiser in 1980 by a local journalist, Ronald Riggs, who was a friend of both the writer and Shaw's last housekeeper, a strict Scottish Presbyterian widow called Mrs Alice Laden. She had been assured by the elderly playwright that there was such a thing as an afterlife, and that he would prove it to her. Some weeks after Shaw's death, he kept his promise by appearing to her twice. The first time she saw him in the doorway of the kitchen, and a few days later she heard his steps on the landing and heard his voice calling, 'Are you there, Mrs Laden?' She said afterwards, 'I was not afraid. I do not question these things, neither am I interested in the supernatural. I only know that Mr Shaw had appeared and that he had spoken to me.'

Such an occurrence would seem to be in character with the eccentric and quixotic playwright's nature. As Paul says, 'My theory is that he is still here, but in a friendly manner.'

'…about forty years ago one of the sisters woke in the night to see a woman dressed in black standing in her bedroom. When asked who she was, the woman turned and walked straight through the wall…'

SHERINGHAM PARK, NORFOLK

The magnificent landscape park of Sheringham was one of Humphrey Repton's most outstanding achievements, and it is popular with visitors who come to admire the woodland garden, the rhododendrons and azaleas, and the stunning views of the Norfolk coast and countryside from the viewing towers. But despite the park's apparent tranquillity, there is believed to be a psychic 'hotspot' centred on a former gamekeeper's cottage, Ivy Lodge, which stands at the main visitors' entrance to the property.

The first unearthly happening at Sheringham is related in *The Banville Diaries*, written by Larry Banville, one of the gamekeepers on the estate in the early nineteenth century. Larry had an unlikely sideline, moonlighting as the local chiropodist. He wrote in his diary that one of his most loyal patients once appeared in the night at the bottom of the stairs in Ivy Lodge, waking Larry up. By the time he descended the man had disappeared, but later Larry discovered that the patient had actually died on that very night when he had been 'visited' by him.

Ivy Lodge was largely destroyed by fire in 1904, but was later rebuilt. The lodge was subsequently occupied by three sisters who were born there in the 1920s, their father having been the gamekeeper on the estate since 1912. About forty years ago one of the sisters woke in the night to see a woman dressed in black standing in her bedroom. When asked who she was, the woman turned and walked straight through the wall. The experience was so inexplicable that the startled sleeper leapt out of bed and rushed to the window, expecting to see the 'woman in black' lying injured on the ground below her window. But there was nothing to be seen.

This apparition may be linked to a tragic accident which had occurred a few years earlier on the estate. During and just after the Second World War, Canadian Forestry Corps workers had been tree-felling at Sheringham Park. A woman who lived at Wood Farm cottage, close to Ivy Lodge, was killed when her bicycle collided with one of the timber lorries on the estate road early one morning. She had been on her way to Sheringham Hall, where she worked. The lady who saw the 'woman in black' that night in her bedroom was convinced that she had, in fact, seen the dead woman cyclist.

SOUTER LIGHTHOUSE, TYNE & WEAR

On a windswept stretch of the north-east coast stands Souter Lighthouse, boldly painted in red and white hoops. It was a technological breakthrough when it first opened in 1871, the first lighthouse to use alternating electric current. For 117 years the lighthouse-keepers of Souter worked tirelessly to warn ships away from the notorious craggy rocks below. Indeed, it seems that at least one of them has never gone off duty…

The lighthouse was acquired by the National Trust in 1989, and from the outset staff have been puzzled by a series of inexplicable happenings. The sounds of running footsteps and slamming doors are frequently heard, particularly in the tower, when the property is otherwise empty. Doors jam mysteriously, and seem to be locked, then easily open moments later.

'It seems to be the case that strange things happen when something a little "out of the ordinary" takes place at the lighthouse – changes to the displays, or unusual events or activities,' comments the current Property Manager. 'It is as if someone – or something – likes to just let us know that we are being watched, or checked…keeping us on our toes….'

The interior of the lighthouse was greatly refurbished in Spring 2002, perhaps the most radical change to its décor and layout in many years. The night before the opening day of the new season, a member of staff was working in the early hours and as he walked into the Engine Room he instantly felt the presence of someone else. He felt – rather than saw – a shadow pass across the floor as if someone was moving behind the air tanks, and the hairs on the back of his neck rose. There was no one else in the room. However, so convinced was he that he actually spoke aloud, greeting the presence, and expressing his hope that it didn't mind the changes made, explaining that they were to encourage more interest in the lighthouse.

Occasionally staff are sure that they have caught a momentary glimpse of Souter's former inhabitants. A new waitress was surprised to spot at the far end of the kitchen corridor a man in an old-fashioned looking uniform, who promptly disappeared. No one else saw him, and no one of that description had come into the lighthouse as a visitor that day.

Around the time of the 'sighting', a number of members of staff commented on the strong odour of burning tobacco in the same stretch of the kitchen corridor, and also in the area around the recreated Keeper's Cottage. Such a smell was inexplicable as no smoking is allowed in the building, and the tobacco was especially pungent. But later the same day, Souter was visited by a gentleman whose grandfather had lived at the lighthouse before the war…and who smoked strong tobacco. This ex-resident was not a lighthouse-keeper, in fact, but a winding engineman at the local coal mine. His company had leased at least two of the lighthouse cottages from Trinity House, then owners of the lighthouse. Over a year later, the grandson paid another visit to Souter, and brought with him some photographs of his grand-parents, parents, and himself as a baby, taken in and around the lighthouse. He was taken into a small staff room near the tea-room, and the visitor and Property Manager sat down at the round table in the middle of the room, facing the window to the north. When he pulled out his sheaf of old family photographs, one black-and-white print showed the heavy-smoking former resident, sitting, facing north, at a round table in the middle of the room… the same pose in the same room, only about sixty years later.

'…The sounds of running footsteps and slamming doors are frequently heard, particularly in the tower, when the property is otherwise empty…'

Staff have become accustomed to inexplicable events at Souter and do not find them threatening, blaming 'Fred the ghost' for anything inexplicable. Items go missing, then reappear in locations which have been checked and checked again. 'Fred' certainly seems to have a mischievous sense of humour – when the Property Manager's friends from London were visiting Souter for the first time, and, as dusk was falling, he led the group up the lighthouse tower via the spiral stairs, one of the party exclaimed and turned round to protest her outrage to whoever had just pinched her bottom. No one was there. She had not known of any of the previous strange incidents at the lighthouse, and was a little taken aback to find herself goosed by a ghost....

'...one of the party exclaimed and turned round to protest her outrage to whoever had just pinched her bottom. No one was there...'

LEFT The outline of Souter Lighthouse and Fog Station at dusk.

'…according to tradition, Lady Mary was so overcome with grief and anger that she picked up her infant son from his cradle and threw him from the window into the moat below…'

SPEKE HALL, LIVERPOOL

One of the most famous half-timbered houses in Britain, Speke Hall seems to have more than its fair share of ghosts. Surrounded by a now grassy moat spanned by an Elizabethan stone bridge, Speke actually started life in the late fifteenth century. It was expanded considerably in the 1530s by Sir William Norris, to make room for his nineteen children, and in 1795 was bought by Richard Watt, remaining in his family until it passed to the National Trust in 1943.

The magnificent black-and-white half-timbered façades contain fascinating interiors spanning many centuries: the Great Hall and priests' holes evoke Tudor times, while the oak parlour and smaller rooms, some with William Morris wallpapers, are evidence of the Victorian desire for privacy and comfort. There is also fine Jacobean plasterwork and intricately carved furniture. A fully equipped Victorian kitchen and servants' hall enable visitors to see 'behind the scenes'.

In the first half of the twentieth century, the family in residence went through housekeepers in rapid succession, all of whom were in a hurry to leave – though they were reluctant to give any reason. All of them stayed in the Ladies' Maid's Room, later known as the Housekeeper's Room, situated in what was the oldest part of the house, on the south end of the servants' corridor on the east side. This room is now part of the staff accommodation so is not open to the public.

The Tapestry Room or Haunted Room is above the Main Entrance on the north side, and was the bedroom occupied by Miss Watt, the last member of the family to live at Speke. The walls were covered with tapestries behind one of which was the door of a cupboard space, to the right hand side of the fireplace. The door had a small catch and the space gave access to the lower stack in the Small Dining Room below, and as such provided an escape route out of the Hall. The room can be visited as part of the winter season 'behind the scenes' tours.

The Tapestry Room is said to be haunted by the ghost of Lady Mary, though the facts are difficult to establish. Mary Norris inherited Speke Hall from her uncle in 1731, becoming an important and desirable heiress. Five years later she married the notorious Lord Sidney Beauclerk, the fifth son of the Duke of St Albans, who was himself the illegitimate offspring of King Charles II and Nell Gwyn. 'Worthless Sidney', as he was called, loved high living and excess so much that eventually he was forced to return to Speke and break the news to his wife that he had frittered away the family fortunes and that they faced ruin and disgrace. According to tradition, Lady Mary was so overcome with grief and anger that she picked up her infant son from his cradle and threw him from the window into the moat below. She then went down to the Great Hall and committed suicide. The story is suitably dramatic but it does not fit the facts – Lady Mary survived her husband by more than 20 years and died peacefully in 1766, while her only son survived till 1781. So the story may well be one that grew out of exaggeration and malice – 'Worthless Sidney' may have had enemies whose descendants chose to make capital of his dissolute behaviour by blackening his reputation.

Nevertheless, the tradition of a ghost at Speke is long-standing. The references to a haunted chamber and the various appearances of a lady in white date back more than a century. One particular story concerns a ghost that is said to have appeared at a dinner party given by Miss Watts. It spoke to her guests and disappeared through a wall.

Staff give credence to the idea that there is some sort of a ghost at Speke; one of them remarked, 'The ghost is not particularly active and seems to be benevolent. Odd things do happen from time to time – there are footsteps in an empty corridor, voices in empty rooms.'

121

'…the father glanced back into the entrance hall and saw Olivia standing halfway up the stairs and looking back at him, still wearing the same dark dress and with her hair pulled back in a chignon…'

SPRINGHILL, CO. LONDONDERRY

A delightfully atmospheric seventeenth-century 'plantation' home, Springhill was once described as 'the prettiest house in Ulster'. For nearly 300 years it was the home of the Lenox-Conyngham family.

The family ghost is a result of a family tragedy. In 1816 George Lenox-Conyngham succumbed to his history of depression by committing suicide, and his second wife Olivia was left to bring up their children. She was distraught and guilt-ridden that she had not been able to prevent her husband's death, and it is her ghost which is believed to roam the house to this day.

Despite this sad story, staff feel that the house has a very happy and tranquil atmosphere and that Olivia is a benign presence, though it can be unnerving to see her walk through closed doors. She seems to be particularly fond of children, having raised six of them herself, and, according to the family legend, she would often appear to the youngest generation in residence.

Some people seem particularly attuned to Olivia's appearances which, unusually, are nearly always in daylight hours. All descriptions speak of a 'perfectly solid', tall dark lady in a black dress, wearing her hair in a bun. One astonished witness, while talking on the phone, saw her sweep through the lobby into the gunroom, the route she would have taken to what would have been her bedroom. On another occasion, the same witness, talking on a different phone extension on an upper floor, saw a lady in an 'old-fashioned dress' pass by him. Perhaps her most dramatic recent appearance was in August 2003, as a family was preparing to leave the house. Just as they were leaving, the father glanced back into the entrance hall and saw Olivia standing halfway up the stairs and looking back at him, still wearing the same dark dress and with her hair pulled back in a chignon.

All of Olivia's appearances have been peaceful and unthreatening, though there is a strange tale associated with the wooden cot that she used for each of her children. During the Second World War, American soldiers stationed at Springhill were disconcerted by the sounds of knocking heard coming from the door of the night nursery. They asked for the cot to be removed, and it was temporarily loaned to the Armagh Museum. The noises stopped, but after the end of the hostilities and the return of the cot, the nocturnal knocking resumed with renewed vigour.

ST MICHAEL'S MOUNT, CORNWALL

St Michael's Mount is a striking islet of granite that rises abruptly from the level sands – or, at high tide, the waters of Mount's Bay. A mysterious, ancient, romantic place, it has long been the source of stories of saints and soldiers, pilgrims and pirates. Legend states that an apparition of the Archangel Michael appeared to fishermen here in 495AD to warn them off the rocks, foreshadowing the founding of the monastery and place of pilgrimage.

In the 12th century the Abbot of Mont St Michel in Normandy – which bears a striking resemblance to its Cornish namesake – established a Benedictine priory on the island. The castle that crowns the 70-metre (230ft) mount dates from various periods; parts of the masonry can be traced to the original priory buildings, while the entire south-east wing was built in the 1870s by a cousin of the St Aubyns, the family that acquired the island in 1659 and still lives in the castle today.

The Mount is also associated with the Cornish legend of the Giant Cormoran and Jack the Giant-Killer, a story which bears an uncanny resemblance to the fairytale 'Jack and the Beanstalk'. The tale goes that the Mount was built by the giant Cormoran, who was feared and detested by the locals because he made regular forays to the mainland to steal their livestock. One night a brave young man named Jack rowed out to the Mount and dug a deep pit in the hillside while the giant slumbered. At sunrise Jack blew his horn to wake the giant. Blinded by the sunshine, Cormoran careered down the side of the Mount and fell to his death in the pit. A well in the hillside is still shown to young visitors to the Mount as the pit dug by Jack the Giant-Killer.

OPPOSITE A panoramic view of the twelfth-century castle on St Michael's Mount.

'…The tale goes that the Mount was built by the giant Cormoran, who was feared and detested by the locals because he made regular forays to the mainland to steal their livestock…'

ABOVE *The world-famous monument of Stonehenge has been revered for centuries as a place of immense spiritual significance.*

'Pile of Stone-henge! so proud to hint yet keep
Thy secrets, thou that lov'st to stand and hear
The plain resounding to the whirlwind's sweep,
Inmate of lonesome Nature's endless year;
Even if thou saw'st the giant wicker rear
For sacrifice its throngs of living men,
Before they face did ever wretch appear, Who in
his heart had groaned with deadlier pain
Than he who, tempest-driven,
thy shelter now would gain.'

WILLIAM WORDSWORTH, SECTION XIV 'GUILT AND
SORROW; OR INCIDENTS UPON SALISBURY PLAIN'

STONEHENGE DOWN, WILTSHIRE

Massive and mysterious, Stonehenge was already ancient before the Romans arrived. The monument itself is now in the care of English Heritage, while the National Trust looks after 900 hectares (2,225 acres) of surrounding downland and farmland, to preserve the fine Bronze Age barrow groups, believed to be burial mounds, the Avenue and the Cursus, thought to be an archaic processional way.

Unexplained phenomena have been recorded across the whole site. One story dates back to August 1971, a time when the stones were fully open to the public (today access to the monument is limited, to protect the site from damage). A group of hippies decided to camp out in the centre of the stone circle, pitching tents and laying campfires. A violent thunder-storm erupted at about 2am. At the height of the storm, two witnesses, a farmer and a policeman, were shaken to see an eerie blue light illuminating the stones so brightly that they had to avert their eyes. Both men heard screams from the campers, so they each rushed to the monument, expecting to find people injured, perhaps having been struck by lightning. But when they arrived the makeshift camp was deserted – all that was left were the ashes of the fire and a number of smouldering tent pegs. The hippies, so the story goes, had simply vanished into thin air.

There are many strange stories associated with the surrounding landscape. Staff living and working at Kings Barrows Ridge have been at a loss to explain strange blue flashes occasionally seen arcing across the barrows with a simultaneous loss of electrical current. There is a large number of burial mounds and they dominate the area, individually or in groups. A few are isolated, standing proud above farmland, but others lie partially concealed in woodlands and are popular with walkers.

One intriguing tale dates from the late 1950s. On an autumn evening a local man was walking along the barrows in the woods, near King Barrows Ridge. He became unsure of his direction as dusk enveloped him, so he climbed to the top of a barrow, from which he spotted some lights in the distance. Assuming they were signs of a house or road, some landmark to help him regain his orientation, he descended the barrow – only to see the lights coming towards him. What he had thought were electric lights were actually flaming torches, and he felt certain that they were being carried by a group of modern-day Druids, enacting some pagan ritual. Not wishing to be seen, he hid behind a tree as the procession passed him, then quietly followed, presuming that they would eventually lead him to a main road. He described the figures as appearing to be wearing hoods of some sort, but walking noiselessly.

The procession reached the edge of the wood and the thankful walker, not wanting to make himself known to the group for fear of disturbing them, took a shortcut onto a familiar path and glanced behind him out of curiosity. As he watched in horror, one by one the torches went out and the figures disappeared into thin air. Whatever he had seen, the figures in the silent procession were not of flesh and blood.

Investigations have shown that the edge of the woods around the King Barrows is part of the Avenue, the processional way to Stonehenge. It is likely that people of the Bronze Age saw the much earlier edifice of Stonehenge as a place of divine power and sanctity, so chose the locale as a burial site for successive generations of kings. So perhaps the lost walker had inadvertently followed a funerary procession from thousands of years ago.

'…The hippies, so the story goes, had simply vanished into thin air…'

'...yet if she entered the room alone in the evening, her skin would instantly become clammy and her hair would stand on end...'

STOURHEAD, WILTSHIRE

The splendid landscape garden of Stourhead was laid out by Henry Hoare II between 1741 and 1780, with constantly changing vistas around a lake, Classical temples, a stone bridge, a cascade, a thatched cottage, and a grotto. But the ghost story connected with Stourhead emanates from a more prosaic part of the estate. The Education room is situated in an outbuilding, probably a former tack room, in the same courtyard as the Spread Eagle Inn. It backs onto the graveyard of the fourteenth-century church of St Peter's, and the windows look out onto the Memorial Hall.

The Education room used to be the National Trust's shop at Stourhead. At the time shop staff did not report any ghostly activity, perhaps because they only used the premises in daylight and seldom worked there alone. When the shop relocated to a larger site, the two-storeyed complex was converted into a large room suitable for accommodating school groups and family events. The space was also subdivided on the ground floor by sliding glass doors to create a small kitchen on one side and a classroom on the other.

The Education Co-ordinator at Stourhead was greatly involved in the conversion, and she began to notice odd sensations as the work progressed. Nothing unusual would happen in daylight, yet if she entered the room alone in the evening, her skin would instantly become clammy and her hair would stand on end. On one occasion, when the space was totally empty of furniture, she was shaken by the noise of a massive crash from inside, so much so that she felt the room reverberate. She was the only person with a key to the premises, and would often unlock the door to carry boxes in or out, then find it had been locked again before she could complete the task. Objects would be moved or disappear entirely, only to reappear several days later in the most unlikely places, and one set of electrical lights in the main room repeatedly failed, although tests revealed that there was nothing wrong with the supply or fixtures.

The Education room opened in March 2003, and school groups and other parties regularly used the facilities during daylight hours. One evening, as the Education Co-ordinator walked into the room, she had the familiar sensation of her hair standing on end, and of feeling icy-cold. As she stared in disbelief, a grey figure floated out of the back wall, advanced slowly across the floor and drifted out through the window into the courtyard. The figure was roughly human in shape, but too indistinct to be identified as either a man or a woman. The wall from where the wraith had appeared backs onto the graveyard – indeed the floor-level of the Education room is three feet below the level of the ground in the churchyard. Surprisingly perhaps, the witness wasn't frightened by the apparition, though she certainly hadn't expected to see anything. 'I am never spooked by it, whatever it is,' she comments.

STOWE LANDSCAPE GARDENS, BUCKINGHAMSHIRE

Europe's most influential landscape gardens have inspired writers, thinkers, artists and politicians from the eighteenth century to the present day. At the centre of the 100 hectares (250 acres) of gardens, lakes, wooded valleys and landscaped vistas is Stowe House, now Stowe School. In the grounds are more than 30 temples and monuments, including the famous Palladian Bridge, scene of a gruesome accident and a related ghost story.

Built in the late 1730s by James Gibbs, the covered bridge was intended as the main route for coaches approaching Stowe House from the Bellgate entrance. But the bridge was tricky to negotiate, being narrow and only 8 feet high above the road surface – to this day, visitors can see chips and gouge marks inside the structure where vehicles have scraped against the stone. On one occasion an aristocratic lady visitor to Stowe realised with alarm that her coachman was driving the horses too fast as they approached the bridge. She shouted out to slow down, but he couldn't make out what she was saying her and leant down to hear better – and at that instant the coach struck the bridge. The unfortunate coachman was killed outright. Horrified estate staff ran to the scene and managed to calm the horses and rescue the shocked lady passenger.

In the mid-1940s, two unflappable house-matrons at Stowe School were taking an early evening walk together at the top of Hawkwell Field, which overlooks the Palladian Bridge. Suddenly, they both experienced a sensation of panic and alarm, and out of the dusk they saw two highly agitated figures in eighteenth-century dress running towards the bridge as though in alarm. The figures vanished as suddenly as they had appeared. On their return to the school the mystified house-matrons were told about the calamity which had happened at that spot more than two centuries before.

SUTTON HOUSE, LONDON

This Tudor building in the centre of Hackney in East London appears to have a lively night-life. There have been reported sightings of a lady in long white clothes, first spotted by one of the workers of the trade union that was based at Sutton House from 1970 to 1982. The union official came into work early one morning and saw the White Lady glide past the door of the room that is now the shop. The official stepped outside, to ask if she could be of assistance, but there was no one there. In the late 1980s a photograph of a group of friends at a birthday party was taken in front of the café bar, and when the film was developed, a white figure with outstretched arms could be seen standing in front of them.

At night, dogs have been heard wailing inside Sutton House. These are thought to be the dogs of John Machell, a wealthy wool merchant and Master of the Clothworkers company who lived in Sutton House from 1550 to 1558. The dogs can be seen in the coat of arms found in the fireplace in the Little Chamber. Visiting dogs to Sutton House have been known to stop at the foot of the painted staircase, transfixed, and unable to go any further. John Machell was succeeded by his son, another John, who lived in the house until 1605 and whose wife Frances died there in 1574 while giving birth to twins. It is thought that the White Lady could be Frances, looking for her children.

While Sutton House was being restored in the early 1990s, an architectural student living in the House reported waking up one night in the room that is now the exhibition room and seeing a lady, dressed in blue, hovering above his bed. A recent house steward at Sutton House also encountered the Blue Lady when he awoke to find her violently shaking his bed. It is thought this could be the ghost of Mary Tooke, who died there in 1750.

Shortly after these apparitions, a séance was held at the house by local spiritualists; they claimed to find many spirits in residence, most of them benevolent, except for two known as Tim and George, between whom there appeared to be a great deal of bad feeling. By coincidence a local historian, Mike Gray, had been examining public records relating to the house, and only a few days before the séance (but before he had had time to tell anyone of his findings) he had discovered that in 1752 – when Sutton House was divided into two parts – one half was rented to a Timothy Ravenhill, and the other to a George Garrett. In fact, they were the first rate-payers to be registered in the newly divided properties in 1752. Timothy and George were both silk weavers and Huguenots, French protestants, a number of whom have lived at Sutton House through the ages. According to the spiritualists, Tim and George were an unhappy pair, prone to bickering and arguments, and each may have regarded the other as 'the neighbour from hell'.

'…A recent house steward at Sutton House also encountered the Blue Lady when he awoke to find her violently shaking his bed…'

Perhaps the reports by staff and volunteers of occasional poltergeist-type activity at the house, such as sudden drops in temperature, the doors of cabinets opening of their own accord, or objects like candles and noticeboards flying across rooms unaided, are a manifestation of the long-standing enmity between the pair.

'...he leapt from his ladder and backed into a corner of the cellar, watching in disbelief as the trumpet-player emerged through the wall, marched across the cellar and disappeared into the opposite wall...'

TREASURER'S HOUSE, YORK

York is the leading contender for the title of the most haunted city in Britain, with at least 140 ghosts recorded at various locations around the ancient city. The Treasurer's House, built over the main Roman thoroughfare leading into York, was featured in the *Guinness Book of Records* for having the 'Ghosts of the greatest longevity'. There has been a building on the site for over two millennia. The first Treasurer of York Minster, Radulphus, took up residence around 1100. The house was destroyed in the great fire of York in 1137, but was later rebuilt on the same site, incorporating parts of previous buildings. It was subsequently altered in both the sixteenth and seventeenth centuries.

A large number of people have reported seeing the ghosts of a Roman army in the cellars of Treasurer's House. Perhaps the best-known account is that of Harry Martindale. Now a retired policeman, Harry at the age of 18 was an apprentice heating engineer. In 1953, he was installing central heating in the cellars when he heard the sound of a trumpet and saw the top of a soldier's helmet apparently emerging from the wall against which he had just been working. He leapt from his ladder and backed into a corner of the cellar, watching in disbelief as the trumpet-player emerged through the wall, marched across the cellar and disappeared into the opposite wall. Following him plodded a horse, then about twenty soldiers walking two abreast – curiously, they all appeared to be walking at a lower level than the floor on which Harry was standing. The sound of the trumpet continued as the soldiers filed past the young engineer carrying lances, round shields and short swords. According to Harry, they looked very tired, rumpled and dirty. He fled upstairs and ran to the museum curator who remarked 'By the look of you, you've seen the Romans, haven't you?'

Following Harry's experience, there was much debate about the detail he was able to provide as to the soldiers' appearance and kit – it was believed at the time that the Roman infantry carried rectangular rather than circular shields. But later research revealed that during the fourth century the Sixth Legion was withdrawn from York and replaced by auxiliary troops who did in fact use distinctive round shields.

Harry was not alone in his Roman visions – just after the Second World War the then curator had a similar experience, and in the 1930s the soldiers appeared to an American academic. While the house was in private hands in the 1920s, the owner, Frank Green, held a fancy-dress party and one guest was amused to find herself in the cellars with a man dressed as a Roman soldier who barred her passage by placing a spear across the corridor...she was less amused to discover subsequently that not one of the guests had come dressed as a Roman soldier.

Interestingly, archaeological excavation of the site was to reveal a Roman road known as the Via Decumana, leading from the north-eastern gate of York to the legion's headquarters, located about 18 inches below the floor level of the Treasurer's House cellars. An excavation trench had already been dug by the time Harry tackled the central heating, so as the soldiers passed that spot he was able to see their sandalled feet – he also recalled that it looked as though they had been cut off above the knees. Intriguingly, the route they were following appears to have taken this tired and dishevelled troop of soldiers *away* from their barracks – so had they been routed at some skirmish but sent out again to engage an enemy attacking from a different direction? And is there any link with the famous 'Lost Legion' who disappeared without a trace?

'…he was startled to hear the disembodied voice of the young chorister…'

UPPARK, WEST SUSSEX

Uppark is a fine late-seventeenth century house situated high on the South Downs, with magnificent views towards the Solent. It houses an important collection of paintings, furniture and textiles formed by members of the Fetherstonhaugh family, and is set in attractive grounds.

The estate is a magical survival from the Age of Enlightenment and its attempt to achieve a seamless blend of nature, art and architecture, while the house has been lovingly restored following the devastating fire of 1989. As befits such a magical place, there are a number of ghost stories associated with it. One architectural historian recently showed a Cuban historian around Uppark, and the visitor saw two female ghosts in the basement. 'He could describe the print of the women's dresses exactly,' reported the architectural historian. 'None of the rest of us saw them, but he was very quiet in the car on the way home.'

The Red Drawing Room is said to be haunted by the ghost of Sir Harry Fetherstonhaugh (1754–1846), whose portrait as a young man on the Grand Tour by Pompeo Batoni still hangs above the fireplace. Sir Harry was a fascinating character and in a long life packed with incident had an affair with Emma Hart (later to become Emma Hamilton and mistress of Lord Nelson), was close friends with the Prince Regent, and in his seventies married his dairymaid, Mary Ann Bullock. Sir Harry is said to be very particular about the layout of this room; staff have been mystified on finding a firescreen reversed if it has been deliberately left in the wrong position in front of the fire, and on hearing noises in the room when they know the house to be otherwise empty.

Sir Harry is also associated with a well-known local ghost story, related to a hunting lodge on the estate. In the early nineteenth century, a family wedding was to be held in St Mary's Church, and the newly completed hunting lodge was to be the scene of the wedding breakfast. A great many aristocratic guests were expected, including the Prince Regent. The night before the nuptials, the choir held one last practice session at the hunting lodge, and after everyone else had dispersed, one of the young choristers overheard a small group of men plotting a murder. Details of the plot are vague – some believe it was to be an attempt on the life of the Prince Regent, others that it was an act of revenge against Sir Harry for sacking a number of his estate workers. The chorister was discovered by the plotters, who killed him to prevent him warning anyone, and concealed his body on the Downs.

The following morning, the vicar who was to officiate at the wedding ceremony was preparing the church when he was startled to hear the disembodied voice of the young chorister telling him of the plot. He alerted Sir Harry, who took a body of men to the stables of the hunting lodge, where they found and arrested the conspirators. One of them broke down in tears and confessed the whole tale – he seemed to be under pressure from an unseen force in the corner of the room to tell the story. The plotters were hanged for murder, and the body of the boy was found on the Downs and interred in St Mary's churchyard. But local people still tell the tale of lights seen in the windows of the old hunting lodge and the smell of fresh flowers lingering in the air, accompanied by the sound of a pure young singing voice.

UPTON HOUSE,
WARWICKSHIRE

Built in 1695 of mellow local stone, Upton House has an outstanding collection of paintings, superb terraced gardens – and a mysterious ghost. An invisible intruder stomps across the floor, doors slam, objects rattle, yet these nocturnal disturbances do not appear to affect the highly-sensitive alarm systems.

While staff members at this lovely place claim that, 'Officially no, there are no ghost stories associated with the house,' they can't help but mention the odd experiences they've had while living in the house.

Once, the current Property Manager and his wife were rudely awakened in the middle of the night by the sound of heavy footsteps, and slamming doors, coming from the floor below their apartment. On that level, a sequence of three rooms with inter-connecting doors had been knocked through to create a single gallery in 1927, so the doors they heard slamming had in fact not been there for nearly 80 years. Needless to say, when they investigated, nothing was found to be out of place – but the disturbances that were loud enough to wrench the couple from sleep did not set off the alarms, which were otherwise working perfectly.

The French Room has a 'horrible atmosphere', according to the Property Manager, who has previously worked and lived at a number of National Trust historic sites. The French Room is in the oldest part of the building – the basement has late medieval elements, though the majority of the house dates from the late seventeenth century. The Property Manager does not mince his words: 'I just want to get out of there as fast as I can,' he claims.

And it is not just strange noises that disrupt life at Upton. The staff also notice strong smells of tobacco smoke – sometimes so strong that on more than one occasion visitors have reported a fire at the property. Long and detailed searches have not revealed any signs of a fire and, again, the sensitive detection system remains unactivated. Staff members are unable to account for the source of these strange phenomena.

'I just want to get out of there as fast as I can'

WASHINGTON OLD HALL, TYNE & WEAR

Washington Old Hall is a delightful stone-built seventeenth-century manor house, which incorporates parts of the original medieval home of George Washington's direct ancestors – it is from here that the family surname of Washington is derived.

The Hall has long been reputed to be haunted by a white lady, who was apparently often seen by the families who lived there when it was a series of tenements in the early twentieth century. She was reportedly seen wringing her hands, though no explanation has been suggested for this behaviour. More recent visitors have occasionally enquired about the 'lady in a long grey dress' glimpsed in an upstairs corridor. The more romantic or historically inclined would like to believe the lady is directly associated with the Washington family, but this would be too convenient, and so far no origin or identity for the ghost has been established.

Staff have mixed views about the possibility of the Hall being haunted. Some report 'a few bumps, and smells of lavender', while others have encountered visitors who have described the lady in more detail – as well as a child crying on the staircase. Following a recent wedding at the hall, a small child who had wandered off up the stairs was found sitting on the top step chatting away into thin air. When she was asked to whom she was talking, she replied, 'Oh, just a little girl who was upset.'

A sequence of psychic experiments in 2004 threw up reports of a woodman on the stairs and a child on the landing. And one medium revealed that, whoever the ghost is, she particularly likes to watch the civil marriage ceremonies occasionally performed in the Great Hall. Indeed, a cameraman making a video of a wedding reception in the same room reported to staff that his film clearly showed orbs, balls of white light, around the bride's head.

ABOVE A stone eagle watches over Washington House.

'…following a recent wedding…a small child who had wandered off up the stairs was found sitting on the top step chatting away into thin air. When she was asked to whom she was talking, she replied, "Oh, just a little girl who was upset."'

WICKEN FEN, CAMBRIDGESHIRE

These 240 hectares (600 acres) of fenland, now in the care of the National Trust, are an undrained remnant of the Great Fen of East Anglia which once covered 2,500 square miles (4000 square kilometres). Natural historians judge this wetland site to be one of the most significant in western Europe, as it has more than 300 species of flowering plants growing amongst the reeds, sedges and dense scrub.

As might be expected in a natural environment largely unchanged, there are many stories of the supernatural. For centuries, there have been tales of the Lantern Men, inexplicable lights which flit over the surface of the marshes and meres, and which are believed to be trying to lead the unwary to lose their way, and their lives by drowning in the waterlogged reed beds. Strangers are warned not to whistle in an attempt to keep their spirits up as dusk falls, as the Lantern Men are thought to be attracted by the sound of whistling. In reality, these strange lights are most likely to be caused by marsh gas.

There is a tradition at Wicken Fen that the area is the haunt of a long-dead Roman legion, which has been known to appear for a brief moment to startled witnesses, before evaporating into nothing. In fact, the enterprising Roman occupiers of ancient Britain had managed to carve a canal route from Lincolnshire through the fens, so perhaps their appearance is related to this original transport route.

In common with many other wild and unfrequented places such as Dartmoor, Wicken Fen is reputed to be the haunt of a huge black dog, which stalks through the fens in a menacing manner.

'…there have been tales of the Lantern Men, inexplicable lights which flit over the surface of the marshes and meres…'

FAR LEFT AND LEFT The bleak landscape of Cambridgeshire's fenland lends itself to eerie tales of Lantern Men and Roman Legions.

ACKNOWLEDGEMENTS

The author would like to thank the following people: Grant Berry; Nigel Burnett; Harvey Edgington; Yvonne Osborne; Peter Battrick; Fliss Coombs; Stephen Adams; Sharon Cadman; Claire Bolitho; Shona Owen; Sandra Butler; Barbara Thomas; Paul Faulkner; Charles Crosbie; Leonie Tidd; Vicky Herbert; Ian McCurley; Jane Watson; Bernadette Gillow; Lewis Eynon; Denis Mead; Rebecca Speight; Sophie Blair; Anne Butler; Rodney Shirley; Simon Lee; Beck Lockwood; Michael Claydon; Mike Dobson; Maurica Lavery; Claire Mayle; Emily Hirons; Karen Rudd; Meg Wilson; David Atkins; Sarah Evans; David Kitt; Marcus Halliwell; Paul Boland; Richard Neale; Yvonne Osborne; Robyn Lee; Kate Gardner; Harry Morrison; Adrian Colston; Peter Battrick; Kenneth Anthonisz; Alan Langstaff; Andrew King; Paul Williamson; Helen Mann; Mark Agnew; Graham Crane; Ruth Gofton; Ben Eacott; Scott Green; Bob Hockey; Clare Gogerty; Leila Moore; John Eyre; Lydia Price; Megan Doole; Hannah Jones; Richard Henderson; Robin Mead; Stephen Adams; Jane Ellis; Eilidh Taylor; Tom Whatmore; Simon Osbourne; Michelle Fullard; Janet Clark; Mark Agnew; Michael Thomson; Rachel Hunt; Nick Souter; Linda Griffin; Helen Mann; Helen Lloyd; Hugo Brown; David Atkins; Denise Edwards; Judith Seaward; Les Rogers; Helen Willett; Sam Chidlow; Rebecca Speight; Liz Luck; Richard Wood; Siân Harrington; Ray Sandham; Megan Doole; Ros Daniels; Tim Knox; Simon Marsden; Yvonne Osborne; David Atkins; Nick Winney; Lydia Price; Tony Dawson; Tim Crump; Jeff Cherrington; Lance Railton, The Ghost Club; Alan Murdie, The Ghost Club; Mrs Joyce Rowe; Paul Holden; Paul Williamson; Stephen Adams; Sabina Eberle; Beck Lockwood; Sam Snaith; Laura Moran; Kenneth Grover; Michael Coxson; Charlotte Shute; Margaret Willes; Fiona Screen; Rowan Fitzpatrick; Margaret Gray; Kelly Palmer; Robert Mimmack; Paul Williamson; Jane Ellis.

PICTURE CREDITS

By page order: Cover NTPL/Matthew Antrobus; 1 NTPL/Rupert Truman; 2 and 3 Simon Marsden/The Marsden Archive; 4 NTPL/David Noton; 4 Simon Marsden/The Marsden Archive; 4 NTPL/Andrew Butler; 5 Buckland staircase/George Wright; 5 NTPL/Rod J. Edwards; 5 NTPL/David Noton; 6 Simon Marsden/The Marsden Archive; 9 NTPL/Christopher Gallagher; 10 NTPL/Matthew Antrobus; 12 Simon Marsden/The Marsden Archive; 15 NTPL/Andrew Butler; 16 NTPL/Mark Fiennes; 17 NTPL/Andreas von Einsiedel; 18 NTPL/Rupert Truman; 21 NTPL/Nick Meers; 22 NTPL/Rob Talbot; 24 NTPL/George Wright; 27 Simon Marsden/The Marsden Archive; 28 NTPL Andreas von Einsiedel; 31 NTPL/Andreas von Einsiedel; 32 NTPL/Andreas von Einsiedel; 33 NTPL/Tim Stephens; 34 NTPL/Ian Shaw; 36 NTPL/Andreas von Einsiedel; 38 (t)NTPL/David W. Gibbons 41 NTPL/Matthew Antrobus; 42 NTPL/Andreas von Einsiedel; 44 NT/Steve Kane; 47 NTPL David Noton; 48 NTPL/Rupert Truman; 51 NTPL/Joe Cornish; 52 (t) NTPL/Will Webster; 53 Andrew Butler; 54 NTPL/Andrew Butler; 55 NTPL/Andrew Butler; 56 NTPL/Nick Meers; 57 (t) NTPL/Joe Cornish; 58 to 59 NTPL/Joe Cornish; 60 NTPL/Bill Batten; 63 NTPL/Matthew Antrobus; 64 NTPL/Nadia Mackenzie; 65 NTPL/Nick Meers; 66 The National Trust; 67 NTPL/Michael Caldwell; 69 NTPL/Geoffrey Frosh; 70 NTPL/Nick Meers; 71 NTPL/Nick Meers; 73 Simon Marsden/The Marsden Archive; 75 NTPL/Joe Cornish; 77 NTPL/Nick Meers; 78 NTPL/Bill Batten; 81 NTPL/Stephen Robson; 83 NTPL/Nick Meers; 84 NTPL/Joe Cornish; 87 NTPL/Ian West; 88 NTPL/Matthew Antrobus; 93 NTPL/Paul Kay; 94 NTPL/Nick Meers; 97 (t) NTPL/Andreas von Einsiedel; 98 to 99 NTPL/Nick Meers; 100 NTPL/Peter Cook; 101 NTPL/Peter Cook; 102 (t) NTPL/Matthew Antrobus; 104 to 105 (t) NTPL/Matthew Antrobus; 106 NTPL/Andreas von Einsiedel; 107 NTPL/Andrew Butler; 108 to 109 NTPL/Andreas von Einsiedel; 110 (t) NTPL/Dennis Gilbert; 112 NTPL/Joe Cornish; 114 (t) NTPL/Matthew Antrobus; 118 to 119 NTPL/Matthew Antrobus; 121 NTPL/Geoffrey Frosh; 122 to 123 (t) NTPL/Matthew Antrobus; 124 to 125 Simon Marsden/The Marsden Archive; 126 Simon Marsden/The Marsden Archive; 128 to 129 NTPL/Stephen Robson; 130 NTPL/Rupert Truman; 132 NTPL/Nick Meers; 135 (t) NTPL/Matthew Antrobus; 136 (t) NTPL/Nadia Mackenzie; 137 NTPL/David Tarn; 138 NTPL/Rod J. Edwards; 139 NTPL/Nick Meers; Back cover: NTPL/Nick Meers; NTPL/David Noton; NTPL Andreas von Einsiedel; NTPL/Matthew Antrobus; NTPL/Matthew Antrobus.

Simon Marsden's images can be seen at www.marsdenarchive.com

First published in the United Kingdom in 2006 by

National Trust Books

1 Gower Street

London WC1E 6HD

An imprint of Pavilion Books Company Ltd

ISBN: 9781905400379

A CIP catalogue record for this book is available from the British Library.

Layout design by Neil Stevens and Bet Ayer

Cover design by Lee-May Lim

15 14 13 12 11 10 9 8

Colour reproduction by Master Image, Singapore

Printed and bound by Craft Print International Ltd, Singapore